I0535171

SOLUM JOURNAL
VOLUME VI: Doubt

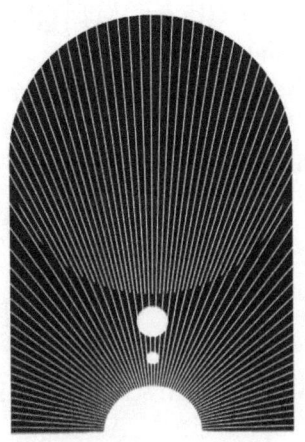

SOLUM JOURNAL
VOLUME VI: DOUBT

AN IMPRINT OF SOLUM LITERARY PRESS

Solum Journal is an annual literary journal. It is a project of Solum Literary Press, a Christian small press publishing poetry, fiction, and homilies.

MASTHEAD

Riley Bounds, Publisher and Editor in Chief
Christine Pelliccio, Managing Editor
Douglas J. Lindquist, Content Editor and Theology Editor
Elizabeth Genovise, Fiction Editor
Sarah Christolini, Graphic Designer
Emma Winchell, Social Media Editor and
Substack Coordinator

SOLUM LITERARY PRESS

2205 W Broadway Ave. A-119
Anaheim, CA 92804
(480) 371-9053
info@solumpress.com

All rights reserved. No part of this publication may be reproduced in any form without the prior written permission of Solum Press editorial staff, except in the case of quotations in critical reviews or other noncommercial uses permitted by copyright law. For permission requests, email the publisher at info@solumpress.com with "Attention: Permission Request" in the subject line.

For submission guidelines, purchasing, and subscription information, please visit https://www.solumpress.com.

ISBN 978-1-965169-08-7
ISSN 2996-3370

Readers
Abbi Bodager
Rosa Lía Gilbert
Grace Crall Giles
Claire Hellar
Theresa Zoe Williams

Copyeditors
Grace Gilfert
Stephanie McGuire
Amber B. Mullinax
Karah Snyder
Hanna Trainor
Steven Wierenga

Contents

SHORT STORIES

HOMILIES

CALL TO PRAYER

Caroline Liberatore

Apparitions

Has it all been my imagining: the split-second green
that bejewels the setting sun, sparing a conspiratorial wink

only for the attentive? I find it almost obscene that
when a bird supposedly flees from a tree, it leaves

the branch wagging its finger, as if scolding: *look more closely.*
Were the river droplets teasing a trail back to a fish

having just vanished from periphery? I grieve the wishes
just missed by comet remnants, and my eyes, again, blanketed.

Caroline Liberatore is a writer, editor, and librarian based in Cleveland, Ohio. Her vocational pursuits are indicative of what she cares most deeply for: the written word, artistic and intellectual excellence, embodied presence in local communities, commonplace beauty, and redemption as articulated in the tangible, reconciling work of Christ. Caroline currently serves as Editor at *The Clayjar Review* and writes regularly on her Substack, Dog-Eared Inquiries.

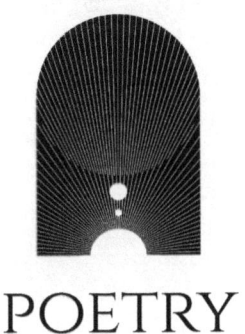

POETRY

ALEA PEISTER

FEATURED POET

Evensong: Bolsa Chica State Beach

Sometimes, Father, it is easy to believe
you are good. A warm night covers
the beach. The sand is calm
under my palms and ankles. I feel
its silky print on the pads of my fingers.

A breeze glides past my face and neck.
I listen to the surf's steady, crashing
breath. I press my fingers
into the calmness of this earth.
The Palisades Peninsula glitters

like a girl's skirt draped
over a pile of laundry. I stand,
peel off my socks, hike my pants
over my calves and wade into the water.
Its cold touch startles, turns warm,

recedes, returns cold, reminding me,
somehow, of a kiss. Oil rigs
and airplanes twinkle in a hazy sky.
I turn my face to the cool pressure
of the breeze, breathe deep, and find

I am glad of this darkness.
So it is, Father, that sometimes
silence pulls close. Even though
most days silence
is behind my most persistent

desolations, sometimes it is
silence that makes it simple,
even easy, to believe you are good.

Dim Witness

Be still, and let the dark come upon you
Which shall be the darkness of God—
    —T.S. Eliot

   1. Seven (Rye, NH)

There is a silence
in the space that gapes
over a snow-laden rooftop: flakes
of dim witness still falling,
the air so cold it holds
a kind of sweetness.

My sister sleeps. I reach
over her deep
breathing, ease
the gabled window open, grasp
one more palmful of snow.

Silence hits me with the cold.
I taste its gush
through the crack—my nose
gone pink so fast—spit pooling
in the hollow beneath my tongue.
Drops of melted snow
go warm on my fingertips.

Unknowable—
enclosed—ringing—how
that silence seems—

2. Twenty-eight (Humboldt County, CA)

A congregation of
of redwoods presses close
against the road's lips
in the dark.
Trees, road, stones—save
what I glimpse
in the passing flash
of headlights all
are darker than night but the sky
is star-strewn, slightly more blue.

I drive with windows
tight-shut; hear car tires
rumble over asphalt; hit *play*
on the stereo. In the sudden weight
of my solitude I only want
a lover's body here, with me

—but
to see the darkness
of these redwoods
is to see the expanse
of their silence. The same
silence. And I again its witness.

Desert Body

Temperatures rose. At noon this desert
felt one-hundred-degree heat. It was only spring.
Outdoors, my head hurt. My body felt weak.

I stayed inside most of the time looking
through windows at a landscape like skin.
Beige hills. Brown stones and shadows. Rough
honey-colored boulders. Broad swaths of sand.

The hills sat low on the horizon.
The hills were like a naked woman reclining on her back or side.
The hills were like my body naked
on cool bedsheets

alone. I did not know what to do with my body.
I did not know what my body was when its ache
became a flood I could not dam or navigate,
became a need that wounded me.

I prayed in the desert. I begged you to seek out
and find me. I did not know if you were God or a man
but I wanted your touch. I begged you to never forget me.

When At Last Rain

When at last rain comes it comes at night,
stealing over cracked soil as I sleep. After days
and days of biding time, of opaque skies,
I wake to absence. Drops of water drip

from eaves. Driveways gleam. Opalescent
motor oil swirls in potholes, asphalt cracks,
concrete seams. Birds twitter about their business.
Everywhere pervades a smell like cold money.

This parched earth opens

as it can to the torrential touch of fleeting rain
but its need is too great, its need is greater
than what water comes. Water runs
off soil in streams.

        And my soul in prayer
is this desperate earth. And Your presence
is the rain.

Pantoum for Eucharist, Advent

You ask God why the gift of His love is a silence
because you, knowing, don't comprehend why.
You don't remember how to hold a child.
What is it your hands forge and forget?

Because you, knowing, don't comprehend why
you try to find better thoughts.
Whatever it is your hands forge and forget
you might not go back next time.

You try to find better thoughts.
You go to church, you eat Him, you eat the Christ Child —
you might not go back next time.
You eat Him. You wonder: *Does He remember me?*

You go to church. You eat the Christ Child.
You are troubled when you try to hold a child but you clutch
and you eat Him and you wonder *does He remember me.*
You ask God *why the gift?* His love is a silence.

Alea's writing has been featured in *Relief, Solum, Ekstasis, The Curator, The ClayJar Review, Vita Poetica, Whale Road Review,* and *Art for the Isolated,* among others. In 2025, she will graduate with an MFA in Spiritual Writing from Seattle Pacific University. Alea is passionate about the relationship between creativity and prayer, which she explores in ministry at her church. She daylights as a copywriter at a marketing firm. You can follow her writerly escapades on Instagram at @alea_peister and Substack at aleapeister.substack.com.

LAURA HOWARD

In Between the Rooster and the Dove

He looks up at me from that log like
we're on solid ground. He always has been.
But I said no to his name without the kind of
second thought I gave the waves.
Nobody even paid me for it.

He cuts open the fish I bring him. I too swam here,
am trapped in a net. Come eat breakfast. Maybe this time
he'll make enough for leftovers. Simon,
do you love me? I'm on the ground now, legless,
gasping through gills. Yeah, I love you.

The third time's a knife. He touches my arm and
I see what he can: net at my feet. Brother,
your breakfast isn't getting any warmer.
In forty days I'll be a bird, regurgitating this meal
onto someone else's tongue.

Laura Howard is a writer based in Wheaton, Illinois. She holds a BA in Philosophy and Biblical & Theological Studies from Wheaton College and an MDiv from the University of Chicago. Laura's work has appeared in Ekstasis Magazine, Christianity Today, and *BitterSweet Monthly*. You can find and follow her work at her Substack: Let Me Be Heavy.

OLLIE BURGESS

when saints die

(a train of thought while staring at an ikon of St. George,
who coldly stabs the metallic skin of the sea beast.)

sometimes the night is not the absence
of light but a Thing like an unsheathed sword.
I sit, in the beam of a full and yellow moon,
facing the irritating luster of gold-veneered ikons.
this, this is when the saints would whisper prayers
and wait for you to pierce them with a spear.

yes, my words should gain their bravery and tiptoe
out of the cavern of my lips, but silence is safer.
it avoids conjuring up the beastly things
you let wallow beyond the vault of the clouds,
avoids incantations that would pick apart
the rungs of my DNA with deft fingers.

if I ventured beyond the mouth of the cave,
you would capture me, make me a prisoner
of war, like all those saints who stared down a lion's
throat. all these saints sit illuminated, gilded,
hypothetically harmless on my wall. how many
of them left this world without tattered and bloody clothes?
is your fingerprint not dipped in their blood?

you caught them in the beam of jaundiced light
and whispered ethereal things into their bony minds.
when Leviathan got sleepy eyes, they ambled
close until his nostril-breath lifted their hair.

the beast was quick and clawed them apart
the instant they lifted their sword. where are they
now? in heaven, as the bishops predicted,
or in hell, where the pagans banished
them so they could have some peace?
all cultures after all believe incompatible things.

you could be the world's greatest cheat, God,
for even saints' minds lie. maybe when saints die
they have the feeling I'm having right now:
that all your miracles are placebo pills we swallow
just to make us feel like we're not unraveling.

blood drips from your spear. perhaps it really is
as the tales say, and it's real dragon's blood.
but step on my side of the window pane and see
what I see: bloody swords in the *hands* of some saints,
and in the *chests* of others, and an ikon, in which you
are St. George, and I the dragon.

Ollie Burgess is a piano teacher who lives in a small town west of Atlanta. When she is not writing poetry, she is either reading, cooking, talking theology, or gazing at the stars. She posts poems on her Substack, Olivet Poetry (olivetpoetry.substack.com).

LILA ROBINETT TINDALL

All Shall Be Well

After Julian of Norwich

I told myself not to ask

                                     for wisdom anymore, not
                 for humility, not for love
                                       to make its way
                                     to anyone, or me
nor for anyone's face to be turned
                         upward, inward, toward.
                               If I wanted to know
if Christ would bring me
                 back home I had to believe
in the void   & there's no point
       in thinking   into a void. I had to believe
that prayer was nothing but thoughts
                               and thoughts are nothing but
spaces in between branches, the wind
running in between.

***

Blood runs between
bone spaces. These careful thoughts
                         are muscles, matter
that grows with sweat,
           not a void where abstractions swallow. I believe
there's no point
                     in going back home I have to believe
Christ exiled me
                             so that I could know

        the brackish movements of turning out, in, toward
the face of the world; everything
                                      to contort
                                    myself, face
           humility, and love
                          for wisdom of bending
open and opening myself to all being.

Lila Robinett Tindall is a PhD candidate at the University of Southern Mississippi where she studies creative writing. She is a native East Texan relocated to Hattiesburg, Mississippi, after graduating with her MFA in Creative Writing from Seattle Pacific University. Her work can be found in *Five South's daily journal*, *Ekstasis Magazine*, and *Vita Poetica*.

TABATHA YEATTS

What Vincent Couldn't See

If I could journey back a hundred and thirty years to visit Vincent,
interrupt him as he sat

composing a letter to Theo or gazing at the sky and seeing brush
strokes there,

if I could speak the truth of the iris shirts and sunflower posters, the
ginger-haired actors

with starring roles, the admiration glimmering like moonlight in a
rainy street, the applause

that travels through the ages steady as a steam engine driving past a
field of grain,

could he believe in a love that never
touched him at all?

Vincent could witness many worlds
others did not see, but not that.

Can a person approach this world
with a faith in love unfelt, unknown?

Not faith that entire museums
 will be devoted to their work,

but confidence in an unknown person
for whom your efforts will be a spark,

someone whose light will catch
by the gentle curve of your flame

leaning across time and space
to ignite.

Tabatha Yeatts is a poet, author, and blogger, as well as the editor of the popular *IMPERFECT* and *IMPERFECT II* anthologies for middle schoolers. Tabatha lives with her family in Maryland.

Emily Neuharth

Faith as Small as a Cherry Seed

"A shoot will spring forth from a stump of Jesse."
Isaiah 11:1, NCB

Our home in Bishkek had a cherry tree
with a swing. Dad would push us while he sang
about us being brave and loved. We'd scream
with delight as fruit fell. We'd fly, hanging
for a moment parallel with the ground.
There was no fear, only Dad's strong arms, pink
blossoms, and sucked-clean seeds we had spat round

the swing. I cast a net in my mind, sinking
into the past. My guard's up, expecting
to catch monsters, but all I find are lips
and hands stained sticky with sugar. Protect
memory from present pain— the eclipse
is over. I let shadowed joy return,
dropping red seeds into my story's urn.

Emily Neuharth currently writes from Chicago, one of her many home-places. She is pursuing an MFA at Northwestern University and loves all that sparkles. Her poetry and creative nonfiction can be found at Solum Press (Summer 2022 and Volume III), *Salon*, and *Petrichor*.

Eric Bodlak

2 Peter 3:10

At sundown, we paddled
out to the overgrown island
whose shores had been off-limits
to us as kids, and slipping through
the briny blackness, I imagined
empty space closing back
around the kayak's hull. Upon

our arrival, we identified then
climbed a tree appropriately structured
for sitting. Sipping beer and watching
the mainland from afar, we saw
that the glimmering constellations and city
lights could hardly be differentiated
in the channel's reflection, and you

asked me, cousin-to-cousin, if
I feared the coming Judgment
of the Lord. But I was never one to believe
in what couldn't be seen, and as the vast
and undulating ocean mass lapped
against the coastline, I knew it was
everything there was. We packed

crushed cans into doubled-up
plastic bags and ferried them
to the landing site, where the waxing
moon appeared to ignite
the sands like cinders scorched star-
white and numinous, and we heard humpback
whales singing somewhere in the dark.

Eric Bodlak is a research engineer who lives and works in Huntsville, Alabama. In his spare time he enjoys playing sports, exploring nature, and reading, writing, and thinking about big ideas. His writing has been published at Cathexis Northwest Press and *Book XI*.

Bethany Jarmul

Don't Look Back
an erasure of Acts 27:13-26 NIV

wind began to blow

                      wind of hurricane force

            i   passed

         the lifeboat

     passed   the ship

afraid   of   the

       violent   day,

the overboard   hands.   stars

    raging, i   gave up

                       an angel

              said,

You must stand before   God

                  God

   told me   run

21

Jesus Storm

an erasure of Mark 4:35–41 NIV

evening came

A furious squall

woke   and said

drown

i   died

it was   calm.

afraid?

ask   Who is   the wind

Bethany Jarmul is an Appalachian writer and poet. She's the author of two chapbooks, including mini-memoir *Take Me Home* from Belle Point Press. Her debut poetry collection, *Lightning Is a Mother*, is forthcoming with ELJ Editions in 2025. Her work has been published in many magazines, including *Rattle*, *Brevity*, *HAD*, and *Salamander*. Her writing was selected for *Best Spiritual Literature 2023* and *Best Small Fictions 2024*, and has been nominated for the Pushcart Prize, The Best of the Net, Best Microfiction, and *Wigleaf* Top 50. Connect with her at bethanyjarmul.com or on social media: @BethanyJarmul.

MEGAN WILLOME

Junco

From Douglas firs winding down,
the Guadalupe Mountains comes
kindness herself. The dark-eyed junco's
song—a mother's cry.

Good rocks hide her nest.
Inside her cup: leaves, grass,
someone's else's feathers,
three pale-blue eggs.

She cannot help herself.
She laments all. She lays
down inside this fossil reef
risen taller than Texas.

If, in winter, you hear her sweet
no-hope notes, when only
weed-seed sustains, trill back
what the darkling thrush sings.

Megan Willome is the author of *Love and Other Mysteries*, a poetry
collection exploring Song of Solomon and the Mysteries of the Rosary. She's
also written *The Joy of Poetry*, a memoir, and *Rainbow Crow*, a picture book
of form poems. Her day is incomplete without poetry, tea, a song, and a walk
in the dark.

Sarah Ashbach

Maundy Thursday

Old women, mothers, families shuffle in,
and though no organ tells us to begin,
we settle on our knees as moonlight strains
the glass of Peter's face. Mother complains
I have not been here since I was a child,
which isn't true. She says the world's beguiled
my mind with doubts—or false security—
but she's the one who somehow cannot see
it is not comfortable within the dark.

I could perhaps try reverence, remark
on all the good that contemplation does,
how lovely and how sad the service was,
when we've gone out to dinner. Across the aisle
a baby's been asleep for some long while
within his mother's arms. She's maybe twenty,
alone, no ring; my mother's cast her plenty
of pitying looks.
        I shift; the kneelers squeak—
my knees respond.
           What is this sad antique
of worship? Grief-stricken in the dark, we wait
to mouth apologies and demonstrate
sorrow to one who might not see us here.
I know the candlelight will disappear—
it always does, of course. Why should I doubt,
as one by one those quickened wicks go out
and cloud the air, the inefficacy
of prayers intoned within a minor key?
Here are our bells, stained glass, and candle smoke:

I wonder whose emotions we provoke.
Surely, not only ours. My mother's laid
her face atop the pew, and in the shade,
I think I see her cry.
                    Candlewax falls.
Our prayers pause. And then the baby bawls
over our quiet profundities. He's right
to suffer, fretful in the candlelight
despite his mother's hushing—as if we care
that he should interrupt our grand despair.
The final canticles and his cries mix
as they snuff almost all the candlewicks
and one last candle hides within a tomb.
The mother's consolation stills the room
until her baby laughs within the gloom.

Half-Sleep

A sailor spoke to me of albatross,
white-winged and flown against the ocean foam,
and when he spoke I felt in me a loss
for lily-watered seas, a hill-side home.
I left, hearing an echo from that shore
like music from a distant chapel bell,
but I can't hear the birds cry anymore,
or trace the song I thought that I knew well.
"Where have the white birds gone?" I ask the wind.
"Where are the gull-roads? Grey ships bowing along
a wave? Where is the shore?" No cries descend
to turn on air and ear, from sound to song.
But once, I heard the white birds sing to me
like bells above the stilled waves of the sea.

Sarah Ashbach is an MFA student with the University of St. Thomas and teaches at a classical Christian school. Her work has been published in *Ekstasis*, *The New Lyre*, and *The St. Austin Review*, and she is this year's recipient of the Frost Farm Poetry Prize.

LAUREN DELAPENHA

The Incredulity
after *The Incredulity of Saint Thomas* by Michelangelo Merisi da
Caravaggio

I grieve
not loss, but the certainty

of loss—even in the miracle of the body
cut open so cleanly, still loss—loss

of certainty, of being the last
to find relief in folded linen

and the words of women.
My grief is urban. I know how it will go.

I will die in a city, people above me and below,
as they wring water, exhausted, from laundry

out the window. Before then, I will cross
a face on the avenue I know as the face

of a lost friend, lost for some simple thing
neither of us remembers.

Which is worse—to mourn a friend who is dead
or alive? Before answering, consider the evidence

of my hand, gnarled from carpentry,
raised now to prod the line open

that I might know horror
and wonder in the soft between one rib

and another and my Lord, my God, my hand
is dirty. My demand—bless me and keep me

dirty, that I would be unrecognizable even
to the pigeons expecting bread

from me. Memory, lift your shirt
that I might hurt, and believe.

The Unhealed at Bethesda

The young try. We lie
in the back, playing backgammon, unclean
as the undead, but beautiful, in our way,
as an artist once said before taking the picture
of our milked eyes, blank teeth, our hilarious
legs. No one has ever been healed
here, but we stay here, swigging stagnant
water the colour of beer. We've been here
a long time. We've learned to finish each other's jokes—
A man walks into a bar—the fact that we stop
mid-sentence to watch the others clamber
over each other like barreled animals
should not be confused with hope
or pity. We laugh at whoever gets there first
and at the rest who don't and can't, won't.
Are we not philosophers who share
a common vision: waiting for something
to happen? Did not the world begin
with water and waiting and the face
of God, who will not suffer
thy foot to be moved?
This, too, sends us, the lame, to tears.

Then, one of the days in one of the years,
a brief kerfuffle, right over there. We are used
to this. A man, they said.
I didn't see him. What I saw was this:
one of us, the lame, walking.
Good for him. It's the ultimate punch
line: to take up your mat and walk
among the lame. For a while, no one talks.
We've been here a long time. It takes
a long time to not believe ourselves divine
comedy. Better, most days, not to think
on such things. Then someone smiles, begins,
A man walks—and buckles, tries again.
A man walks—

Lauren Delapenha is a Jamaican poet and English teacher. She earned her master's in creative writing from the University of Oxford, and her work has received an Oxbelly Fellowship, a Helen Zell, Jamaica Poet Laureate's Young Writers Prize for Poetry, a Grindstone International Poetry Prize, and a Pushcart nomination. Her poems have appeared or are forthcoming in *Relief Journal, The Cortland Review, The Ekphrastic Review, Ekstasis, DMQ*, and various anthologies. She currently lives and teaches in Connecticut. Find more of her work here: https://www.laurendelapenha.com.

JUDE RUETSCHLE

Magpie

Moses saw the magpie
and he wept
for the delight of darkness, the enclosure of light.
And oh, that pagan thrill!
when God asked him to dance his little dance
while God clapped his little hands
and they reclined in the shade—
the anonymity of each others' faces.

God didn't know Moses,
Moses didn't know God,
and their faces shone with light.

Jude Ruetschle is a student of theology and psychology in Spokane, Washington. He drinks copious amounts of tea and convinces himself he is immune to caffeine. He writes, but always too little, and is learning to appreciate the space between words. His poetry has been published in *Ekstasis* and nominated for Bright Wings Audience Choice award.

BRIANNE HOLMES

Silver Shift, Mourning Dress

We stacked doubt
on the pantry shelf
enough to last the winter;
you said yourself
it would be hard and bitter.

All night long, the sea lay howling
at the moon; problems swam in murky pools
and prowled the shoreline in the gloom;
a pinprick of the future stabbed my heart,
pierced my finger, broke my peace apart.

Next day I checked
the pantry shelves and found
some worry missing,
vanished in the night
without a sound.
You said, "I know
exactly who to blame"—
your eyes were boring holes
into the wall behind my ear—
"but I would never
mention any names."
How good of you, my dear,
to misdirect your aim.

Tonight, I'll walk
the ocean's highest tide
while you lurk in the pantry
guarding our supplies.

***

I saw the darkened ocean filled up to the brim
with calendars and empty rooms and rocky fields and ash.

The rising moon became a crown, the waves a silver sash;
the maw of night was velvet, but the roaring sea was grim.

I wish that you were here with me to understand my thoughts,
but you are busy counting all the dangers I forgot.

***

Why do you need, I'd like to know,
that shelf around your neck?
If you forgot it for one day,
would we die of neglect?

And no,
I am not finished yet,
long as the moon remains;
and if you please,
I wish you would
forevermore refrain
from spitting words
with acid laced
upon the window
frame.
This house
is difficult,
you know,

to scour
and maintain.

Tonight, I'll walk the breakers
from midnight until day
while you stand in the kitchen
keeping sleep at bay.

***

The night was clothed in shadows, no light upon the sea;
the mountain clouds obscured the luminescence that we need.
I saw an empty ship sailing strangely close to me
with your silhouette aboard and your shadow roaming free.

And farther down the shoreline was a staircase made of stone;
it was higher than the mountains, it was whiter than our bones.
Your shadow stood upon the height, singing all alone
in a dress of woven starlight, flecked with silver foam.

I never stopped to notice the plummet of your dreams,
and I never paused to hear the murmur of your screams.

***

You look so tired,
wilted, wan
inside this morning light;
your eyes would like to slap me
for welcoming the dawn.

I'll try to start a fire
in this empty, ashy grate;
for kindling I'll use briers
that I weeded by the gate.

I patched the drywall of your dreams—
did you even notice?
Shall I install
new window panes?—
the current view is hopeless.

Tonight, I'll bake
a lullaby entirely from scratch
while you sit on the sofa
and sample every batch.

***

I never wanted much in life and now I want far less,
but words are hard to catch like fish and properly express.

But I will wait—
till the moon has risen on the waves and spreads a shining carpet at
your feet;
then be brave—
run your fingers through the breakers, greet the patient light;
and come—
for you will find no need to stock the shelves, the countertops, the
drawers; and let us be done
with this hoarding of the world—
not because we have plenty, but because we need none.

Brianne Holmes lives in Upstate South Carolina where she works in marketing and communications. In 2016, she earned a Master of Arts in English with a concentration in Creative Writing from East Carolina University. Her writing has appeared in several publications, including the *North Carolina Literary Review, Relief, The Twisted Vine*, the *Journal of Microliterature, As Surely As the Sun Literary, Abandon Journal, Foreshadow*, and *Heart of Flesh Literary Journal*. Learn more about Brianne at brianneholmes.com.

SAM YAZIJI

Hymn from Exile
after the exile of St. Symeon the New Theologian

I watch your noble, arcing wings—
their whirring smites the air and shears
blue holes into the scarf of moonlight
nestling the earth. And my unworthy fingers
touch these flakes of somber snow—
all scattered over looming seaport spires
caressed so sweetly by your feet.

      Why did you come,
      O Fragile One?

Your arcane whisper bears a dour word,
your needling tongue imparts Patriarch's
edict, his fanged command: That I
must spend my days shoeless, alone
at wintry river's edge, staring down
arrowheads so sharp. O Little Dragon-
fly, accept my tears as drops of myrrh
and be my friend for just the time
it takes to flit through frozen Bosphorus
on your gold-threaded wings. Carry
my tears to Him who trampled death
by death, who threw open the doors
of deep pearl and dewy light—
        so that I may never be alone again.

Sam Yaziji is a poet and writer from Miami, Florida. He is currently an MFA student in poetry at San Diego State University, where he works as the production editor for *Poetry International*. His poems have been published in *Zone 3 Press* (forthcoming), *Attic Salt*, and *Passage Prize* Vol. 1. His research interests include Eastern Christian hymnography, wartime poetry, and cybernetics. He is an Orthodox Christian and paints Byzantine icons in his free time.

JOHN DAVIS

Thumbing a Ride

I was hitchhiking with Jesus
   standing under an overpass.
It was so damn hot
   and I said it was damn hot

and Jesus scolded me with his eyes.
   I felt like a sinner
was tempted to pass him the last
   swallow in my water bottle

and said *Jesus, it's hot today*.
   I was waiting for him to break bread
and feed fish to all the motorists
   zooming past, set up a fish barbecue

with hot sauce and minced onions
   hoping one of the drivers with a roomy
sedan, air conditioning, and reclining seats
   would offer us a ride. Maybe his name

would be Moses and we would sing
   spirituals, *Lord Lord Lord*, parting waters
at backed-up bridges, driving on lakes,
   slapping hands or maybe I was standing

under an overpass in one hundred plus heat
   with my scraggly dog. I was out of water
and shadows of the overpass
   resembled a crucifix.

John Davis is the author of *Gigs, Guard the Dead,* and *The Reservist.* His work has appeared in *DMQ Review, Iron Horse Literary Review,* and *Terrain. org.* He lives on an island in the Salish Sea and performs in several bands.

Laura R. McCullough

Honeycomb

My father was a good man.
He was a man split
down the middle,

chasing the thought
of a life. Windows
in tidy rows,
tinted glass and
labyrinths with
no center. He
was terrified of me.

Dangerous; the broad
stroke of a faulty
brush. Walking
like hatred and
spitting curses
to keep Death
at bay, this is
how not to die.
How not to live.

Weak scaffolds
make liars out of
kings, melting down
the remnants
of their crowns
for car keys and
lawn mower blades.

Vigilant, violent

standing in between
paychecks and
paper targets, but
when the snakes
came slinking
through the grass,
no one
was watching.
Double Dutch.
Double life.
Double scoops of
ice cream. Wanting
happy, sweet, bubblegum pink.
But they fed us the bees
instead of the honey.

Climb on my
shoulders to touch
the stars. Count
the grains of sand
your hands won't
keep. See
past the edges
for yourself.
Then bury it.

Go back to work
building nothing and
question
every bitter day. Put
storm clouds
on with your coat and
take them home.
Even hypocrites
can still
find wonder
in created things.

We rise
and fall on
Icarus wings,
etched in wax and
good intentions,
spilling feathers
from a side
pierced by doubt.

Patching leaks while
ignoring the flood,
taught only
to hold the flashlight.
Expected to keep
up as we ran
from failure, their
legs always were
longer than mine.

Powerless now, we
weigh anchor from
their myth, flying
for safe harbor
instead of the sun.
A new torch
lit, to let their
pyres grow cold.
Another side
slit, that mine
might hold.

My Father was a Good Man.
He was a Man split
down the middle.

Laura R. McCullough is an artist and writer happily nestled with her family in the North Georgia mountains. A "lover of faith and believer in what is beautiful," she and her husband work in ministry and music in their community. Laura uses her writing and mark-making to explore how the lyrical power of language can express things we are unable to say. Her work has been published in journals such as *Rattle Magazine*, *The Blue Mountain Review*, *Right Angle*, *Solum Journal*, *Vessels of Light*, *Wild Roof Journal*, and *The Way Back to Ourselves*. Her artwork is featured in several regional museums and galleries.

Haley Schmid

Uncommon Prayer

Some of us require a book of uncommon prayer
with a spine of real bone—the kind of thing
a dog might bury and dig up
and bury again.

Rufus avails himself of a warm afternoon
and trots in, proudly drops '*Lord, it's all feeling
pretty fucked*' on your spotless Persian,
wags his tail.

He knows this is the book you need.
Dogs are good that way.

Cloud Bank

Banked in a mirrored echo
over the Blue Ridge, the clouds
for a span of minutes erased my
doubt's burning rays. The only
admissible thought was 'yes—
here is beauty.' I know my life

is a wisp. Which brows might I
overshadow and briefly cool,
what lovely thing might I expand
by way of imitation? Still quick,
I envy the dead that stand before
the judgement seat and hear

'yes—here is beauty' when God
opens the blue
ridge of his mouth.

Haley Hodges Schmid is an MFA (Poetry) candidate at Seattle Pacific University. She holds qualifications from Hope College, Shenandoah Conservatory, and Oxford University. Her work has been featured in *Cassandra Voices*, *Ekstasis Magazine*, and *Reformed Journal*. She lives in West Virginia with her husband and son.

ALLISON MCFADDEN

Monarch

Up the road, some monarchs sail
and some litter the ground.
They are too far north.
They drift in the dust kicked up
by a three-wheeler.
The orange relics
don't look like the other roadkill,
the ones with the organs mashed into Halloween putty.
The worst is when you slice a yellow finch
and don't know its ending.
A tennis ball skidding up the windshield—
real bones—
and there is a word
for when a thing with a skeleton
crashes into glass
like when a fleet-footed owl
succumbs to
an office window:
it does not
echo down.
Now, the tasseled ends
of a sagebrush leap
into the corner of my eye.
Now, a boy sprints up the road-
gutter in a cape,
chased by a girl
in a cardstock crown,
and my knuckles
are pale
on the wheel.

Allison (Huang) McFadden's poetry has recently been published in *New Verse Review* and *Clayjar Review*. She has also written essays for *Ekstasis* and *Cross + Gavel*. She is a member of Bethel Grove Bible Church in Ithaca, New York.

SHORT STORIES

BROOKE DREGER

What Good Is Any of It Now?

The drug dealer across the street is watering his sunflowers straight from an unnozzled hose. One early spring morning, she'd seen him scatter a handful of seeds against the side of his trailer in that half-asleep way he does everything, with a cigarette hanging loose from his lips, thin flannel pajama bottoms he never seems to change out of hanging low across sharp-skinny hips. At the time, Roberta had wondered where he'd gotten the seeds. She found it hard to imagine him lingering in front of the cardboard displays at Walmart, fingering paper packets as he considered what color would look best against the side of his trailer.

So she hadn't thought anything would become of them; seeds sowed in the dry, yellowed stalks of last year's grass. But they now stand well over seven feet, broad heads bowing in the late morning heat of August, petals a limp burst of flame. She watches him reach up to touch a few of their faces, on his tiptoes as he runs his thumb over their dark cheeks looking for seeds. He flicks at the drooped velvet of its petals with something like dissatisfaction, then drops to his heels and leans over to turn off the tap. As he straightens up, he catches her staring over the rim of her coffee cup.

"Hey, old lady," he says across the street. He throws down the hose, once a bright blue now sun-bleached to a milky turquoise. Water creeps down his driveway, the damp scent contending against the acrid smell of smoke lingering in the air from the fires ravaging up north.

"It's Roberta," she replies.

He takes in his sunflowers again and, with the water still draining from the hose, he asks her, "Hey old lady, you want me to water those for you?" He nods to the plastic baskets of cherry tomatoes that are hanging from her patio; twisted, knobby-kneed vines that are probably too far gone to even pop out a new leaf, let alone a whole

50

tomato. They'd been thriving earlier that spring—but she'd stopped watering them after everything with Mikey, because what was the point?

"No, no thank you, there's no—"

"It's no problem," he says, bending again, the knobs of his spine poking through almost translucent skin. She tries once more to protest, but he's already turned his tap back on, so instead she grips her coffee cup and watches him drag his hose across the street. He cusses at it when it coils up behind him, wringing itself into his driveway like it's digging in its heels, like it wants to stay home. He gives it a yank, arcs the rubber and slaps it against the road to shake it loose. Dust plumes up from the asphalt, a mixture of dry summer dirt and drifting ash. The drug dealer's ribs cut through his shirtless skin when he lurches. But the knot holds tight, inanimately defiant. Finally, grumbling, he walks back over to his side and squats to untwist it, water sloshing across pale feet in plastic slip-on sandals before he gets the sense to kink its neck himself.

Then he's squelching up the three steps of her patio and unkinking the hose over her tomato baskets, soaking them one by one. The plants rise in their pots as the dry dirt floats, suspended for a moment before they sink back into place and begin to drip muddy drops along the wooden railing, stark circles against the peeling white paint. Tutsi, Roberta's Shih Tzu cross, starts to bark from inside. His nails scritch against the metal plate at the bottom of the screen door as he jumps up to look.

"Oh, Tutsi, shush," Roberta chides. From her patio set with the two mismatched chairs next to the door, she cocks a foot out and knocks her bare heel lightly against the metal to rattle him off.

The drug dealer is onto the third basket when a silver truck comes rolling up the road. It stops just before the hose and honks as a window is rolled down. An exasperated arm lifts into the thick air. She recognizes the arm; sharp but indiscernible tattoos weaving up a hairy forearm that belongs to the new guy who just moved into #45.

"Just drive over it," the drug dealer calls, waving the truck on. When it doesn't move, he lets out a frustrated breath and cuts his hand through the air more forcefully, raising his voice as he says, "Drive *over*, for fuck's sake!"

The new guy drives by with his middle finger up, the hose coughing when his tires go over it.

The drug dealer bristles to himself as he finishes up the watering of the fourth basket. Kinking the hose again, he turns to her. "There," he says.

"Thank you." Roberta is eyeing the mess he made, brown water now starting to pool against the porch rug. He doesn't seem to notice. He's pleased with himself and his good deed to an old lady, she can tell by his chest, usually concaved in a slouch but now straight and proud of itself.

He lingers there, switching the hose between his wet hands.

"What, you want a tip or something?" Roberta asks, lifting her coffee cup to her lips.

The drug dealer blinks. Then he shakes his head as he lopes down the porch steps like a kicked mutt. "Whatever, old lady," he mutters. "You're fucking welcome."

There's only so much she can do with her own scant little lawn, with the trailers packed in like they are in Evergreen Crescent. She has a little eight-by-ten space in front, and a slightly larger patch around back that is so shaded by the thick line of hemlocks that separates this park's parcel from the next one over that she's never been able to grow anything back there anyway. Though never much of a gardener, she used to keep a few pots of color along the front of the trailer. But over the last few years, she's let it all go, blaming it on the water restrictions enforced every summer when the province is caught up in flames.

At least that's what she's been telling herself.

So she'd started to fill her lawn with ornaments instead. The first gnome, a hefty ceramic thing, had been slightly sardonic. Was it a cliché to be an old woman with a lawn gnome on the front step? Mikey had teased her, before he'd stolen it, that she was becoming *that* old lady. The plastic flamingo had also been something of a joke; she'd made him stake it into the hard, dry ground for being a smartass—

about something, she can't remember now. Mikey was always a smartass about something. After that, there was the landlocked metal heron with its foot up like the ground disgusted it; a few stone cherubs with smooth little butt cheeks; and a couple whirly doodads that spun technicolor when the wind picked up. It was a gaudy sight, she knew, but she liked it when her neighbors, young moms from #13 and #24 and #19, slowed while herding their kids to the park entrance to wait for the school bus, looking to see if she'd added anything new. She liked it when the park kids stopped by on their bikes and dared each other to fondle the exposed breasts of what had been called a "garden maiden" on the receipt from Home Depot.

This summer, though, there is nothing left except for what is worthless. Just a patch of crusty yellow grass, a crooked flamingo, and those plastic whirligigs, now tattered, having long lost their dollar store glamour. Many evenings she's stepped out onto the porch to get rid of them, but there they stay. She can't decide what is more painful, to get rid of them, or to have to look at them every day. Staking those fluorescent things into the ground earlier that spring was the last thing she and Mikey really did together, the last sort of lucid moment she'd been able to catch in him before things took that turn.

It was during those evenings when she sat on the front steps and watched the whirligigs and thought about Mikey that she caught onto her neighbor's... occupation. Unfamiliar, music-blaring cars pulling into his driveway at all hours of the day and night, weary looking strangers on foot treading unsteadily up his porch steps. If the drug dealer didn't come out and lean through one of the car windows, they went into the trailer, where they either stayed for exactly thirty minutes before heading out the door with their heels on fire, or they stumbled out the front door like vampires into the light of a new morning the next day, lifting a hand to shield their pinhead pupils. Sometimes, when it was late and Roberta couldn't sleep, she'd sit with a cup of tea in the dark and watch these shadow people leave on her neighbors' bicycles, lugging away their propane tanks, stealing away with bulging grocery bags full of goodies as though it were junkie Halloween. They never noticed her, or bothered with her porch. The cheap lawn decorations and the lack of a car must signal her own pension poverty—and besides, Mikey had already taken what was worth anything.

The drug dealer moved in a few weeks after the funeral in May, like some kind of sick tease. A rub in her face. But she'd barely been able to get out of bed then—she kept stepping in Tutsi's shit whenever she got up to finally use the washroom herself—so his arrival had been something of a welcome distraction, despite the company he brought with him. At that time, before she started her walks again, it got her outside, if only to sit on the front steps while Tutsi tiptoed across the new buds of grass, looking up at her with little searching eyes like he was wondering why they never went further than their lot anymore.

"Hey, old lady!" the drug dealer says as he saunters up the street a few days later, shirtless and in those worn flannel bottoms like always. The hems are too long and curled crusty from dragging under his slip-ons. She can see the outline of his cellphone in one pocket and a pack of cigarettes in the other, both heavy enough to weigh on the threadbare fabric. "What are you doing?" he asks, regarding the trailer she's stopped in front of.

"What's it look like?" She lifts the leash connected to Tutsi, who is enamoured with some dark smudge on the curb.

"Nah, I saw you, you've been in front of this place for like, ten minutes. You look fucking creepy, standing out here."

"Oh, shut up."

"Like you're staking out the place."

"I'm not staking anything out," she snaps. "I'm—"

Roberta stops and looks back at the trailer she's been standing in front of. It belongs to Louise Dennis, another long-time tenant like her. Her son's picture is taped in the front window of her trailer, a young man in sunglasses holding up a fish. It's a poster that reads in Comic Sans, "RIP SEAN DENNIS. FENTANYL KILLS. HUG YOUR KIDS IT COULD HAPPEN TO YOU."

Sean Dennis has been up in that window for almost

three years. She's watched his corners curl over time, during all her countless laps around the park with Tutsi while she begged God to do something, wordless prayers she uttered as she watched Mikey leave himself. *Understand me,* she used to beg. *Understand me because I can't—*

But words have come to her now. Roberta has the sudden urge to tear Sean out of that window, the same way she would rip heaven right out of the sky if she could, shred him into little paper pieces like she did to the pages of her Bible to try and escape the language of eternity. Because what good is any of it now? *How in the hell could you let a young man die like that how could you let my grandson die like that look what it's done poster looks like shit is he even there with you I don't know if he had a single thought about you you didn't give me any time didn't even give* him *any time—*

"I'm... praying for them." Maybe praying isn't the right word for it. "For them" isn't even accurate either, but it's not like she can tell the drug dealer she's out here cursing God. "Well, trying to." She glares at him, feeling a soft pull on Tutsi's leash. He's moved on, finally decided on a place to go. He waddles a few steps back onto a neighbor's lawn and eases himself into a squat to pee because he's got old hips like hers. He hasn't lifted his leg in years. "Besides, nothing else to do while I'm waiting for him to shit."

"Can I come with you?"

"Why?"

"I don't know." The drug dealer shrugs. "It's a nice night, kind of. I'm out here already."

"Praying is more of a personal activity," she tries again, hoping he'll take the hint. She can barely stand to look at him, and she can smell him from where he stands a few feet apart from her, like old sweat and cigarette smoke and something bitter. *Scum of the earth,* is the phrase that comes to mind. She holds the end of Tutsi's leash in a tight ball between her hands.

"I'll be quiet," the drug dealer says, watching the trailer. He squints at Sean's poster in the window.

What Roberta doesn't understand is his persistence. He's

55

wasting his time if he's looking for a new customer; she's two steps from the grave already. Seventy-seven this year. But seeing as he's so dead set on accompanying her, and she can think of no other way to get rid of him without using certain words her lifetime in the church would never let her say aloud, she relents as she mutters, "Fine."

They walk in silence. Their sandals, his slip-ons and her foam flipflops, rasp across the uneven, potholed asphalt. The smoke has turned what would be a vibrant evening sky to a hazy peach, the sun a neon red bead dropping behind the Rockies. Even though it's only just become August, the nights are already cooling off. Crickets chirp in the overgrown grass in the median of the park's sardine can crescent, and the trailers at the end of the property lay behind a veil.

"So... how do you know what to pray for?" the drug dealer asks, absently fishing a finger around inside his cigarette pack.

She looks at him, the first time she really has. Rap music drifts from a distant, open window somewhere on the other side of the street. He's about the same age as Mikey, mid-twenties. From here, this close, she can see the track marks up the insides of both his arms, infected red peaks surrounded by valleys of blue.

Roberta swallows, shifts Tutsi's leash to her other hand as he marches off to sniff at the median's curb now. Crickets leap deeper into the grass. "How can you not?" she scoffs, looking away. "You live here, you know this place." Screaming matches through uninsulated walls, hushed conversations at the mailboxes, small talk thrown across the road like a ball, moms hollering for their children across the park the same way she used to holler for Mikey.

"Ah, you're an eavesdropper," the drug dealer says with a short laugh, ducking his head to light a cigarette. "You mind?" he asks as he exhales.

"No, I don't mind, and *no*, I'm not an eavesdropper," Roberta snaps, genuinely affronted. Conversations just don't stop when she appears. No one takes any notice of her. She wanders around this park like she's haunting it. When he continues to look at her with his eyebrows raised, she adds, "Impossible not to be."

He lifts his eyes and surveys the park, nodding with pursed lips. "Yeah, true." He notices her eyeing his cigarette and reaches for his pocket again. "Oh—you want one?"

She lets him ignite it for her, leaning toward the flame of the lighter he holds between them. She coughs when she exhales and catches his look. "It's been a while," she says. "Almost don't need it, with the air like it is." He makes a sound of agreement, taking in the haze around them.

"So what's the deal with this place?" he asks, nodding to the trailer in front of them now.

"If I tell you, you're going to accuse me of gossip."

He laughs. "I promise I won't," he says. "Anyway, I figure two prayers are better than one."

"You're going to pray too?" She sends him the same look he gave her when she coughed on the cigarette.

"Sure." He shrugs, scratching at the side of his neck. "Like you said, nothing else to do while we wait for him to shit."

She sighs. A fat orange tabby sprawls out in the trailer's bay window. "Divorce, here. Ugly. Couple kids in the middle of it."

They stand silently side-by-side, smoking their cigarettes, pretending to watch the dog. She only just gets into her introduction—a tight *God damn you why*—when the drug dealer interrupts her again. "Wait, sorry—I know I said I'd be quiet, but I don't really know what to say," the drug dealer says. "All I've got is some Sunday school shit. 'Our Father who aren't in Heaven,' whatever."

Roberta lets out a breath, and looks up at the drug dealer, at his greasy hair that has started to dread from a lack of care, and the little tattoos scrawled across his chest and down his arms like he gave a four-year-old a Sharpie and told them to have at it. She wonders if anyone out there prays for him the way she prays for Mikey. The right thing to do would be to send one up for him, just in case. But all she can think is *he died because of a piece of shit like this.*

"You can say whatever you want," she tells him, watching Tutsi settle into another squat at the end of a driveway. "Mine usually include a lot of cussing, though, so maybe I'm not the best person

57

to ask."

"Really? Huh," the drug dealer grins, sucks on his cigarette as his eyes drift almost sheepishly up to the sky. "You think it pisses God off?"

"I don't know. Maybe." Roberta tears a poop bag from the little holder shaped as a doggie bone that dangles from the handle of Tutsi's leash. "Sometimes I want it to, when I'm mad enough. Most of the time I just hope he can appreciate the honesty." She nudges the drug dealer's elbow with the plastic. "Do an old lady another favour, will you?"

Roberta eventually stops protesting when the drug dealer drags his hose over to water her tomatoes. He establishes an unpredictable schedule, so she doesn't bother to try and guess when he might come by. Mornings, afternoons, evenings; he starts doing it even when she's not sitting out. She wakes to the sweet incense of wet dirt the mornings he's up before her. And in the evenings while she puts the kettle on, she hears him through the door cracked to coax in some cool air before bed, the water dripping and the drug dealer talking to Tutsi through the screen.

During her walks, she starts being able to squeeze out a half-hearted *do something* for him. Some nights, she fiddles with her whirligigs until he comes bounding down his porch steps, saying, "Old lady, wait up!" She can never tell if he actually prays or if he's just high when his chin drifts to his chest. More often than not, his phone buzzes halfway through, jerking his eyes open, and he has to run back to his trailer, hand raised waving to her as he goes.

One morning at the end of August, he doesn't come to water the tomatoes. A few days go by and she doesn't see him leave the trailer once. Roberta sits on the porch until the smoke makes her head pound. With her sinuses burning, she retreats inside, to sit on the couch with the oscillating plug-in fan turned against her, the one that clicks every time it turns its neck. She tries to watch TV with Tutsi in her lap, but Global and CTV are reels full of the same clips: trees burning, the shells of houses, people living out of their cars in parking lots, tent cities, rising overdoses, people turned into percentages. It all blurs.

It's her pictures of Mikey on the wall behind the TV that remain clear. His brown doe eyes used to wrinkle at the corners like an old man's when he smiled. Somehow the dope made him look younger. It smoothed all his laugh lines, sucked the baby fat he'd been insecure about from his cheeks, pulled his skin so tight around his head that his complexion looked like plastic shrunk in the microwave.

She doesn't have any pictures of him from the last three years, and she's glad she doesn't. He'd shaved away the long, beautiful hair she had spent countless hours brushing and braiding because of the lice he'd caught at the shelter. His eyes had turned wooden, and he'd lost a few of his front-most teeth. Not that anyone would know. He'd stopped smiling by then anyway.

The dog keeps grumbling every time she moves him to get up and pull her curtains from the window to look across the street. Each time she sits back down and looks at Mikey.

Why do I care it could be for the best he's doing it to himself what harm is there one less hand spreading that shit killing our kids he turns men into the kind of boys who rob their grandmothers he's making his own choices so what good is intervening Mikey's dealer that piece of shit I'd go over there I'd strangle that motherfucker myself with my own two hands he deserves it—

He deserves it.

But then she thinks about the drug dealer watering his sunflowers in his pyjama bottoms. She thinks about him wrangling his hose over to her side of the street, and the way he holds out his hand now whenever she reaches for the poop bag dispenser on Tutsi's leash. She thinks of him squatting in front of the screen door, smiling at the dog.

Doesn't he?

She would give anything to be able to cuddle a little Mikey on the couch again, Saturday morning in their own pyjamas while they watched whatever hard-to-follow cartoons made him laugh. That sweet face, with its sweet laugh—someone probably wished he would die too, perhaps after that time he'd been arrested for smashing out all those car windows looking for loose change.

Her tight-lipped repentance looks like jamming her feet into her flipflops and strutting across the dry street cursing God again— *you drive me crazy putting this stupid fool in my life you have a sick sense of humor you know that?*—because she sure as hell is not getting on her knees about it. This is as far as she will go.

"Kid?" She pounds her fist against the metal frame of the screen door of his trailer. "Hey kid, you in there?" She waits a beat and then knocks again, harder this time. "Kid?"

A moment later, the door opens, and the drug dealer emerges from the dark like a spectre; pale, almost see-through. A part of her expects to see his innards through that paper-thin skin, collapsed veins hanging weakly to muscle. There are dark bags under vacant eyes that turn her stomach into a tight knot because *where do these people go?* Recognition flickers some life behind them when he sees her, and they soften as he offers a wane smile at her through the screen. "Old lady, hey."

Stale air drifts through the doorway, smelling of BO and cigarette smoke. Underneath is that tangy, upside-down scent of something rotten. Behind him, the inside of his trailer is dark due to the blankets layered over his windows. In the blue light of his TV, she can just make out the vague shape of someone slumped over on the couch in the main room, a coffee table cluttered with the shadowed forms of cans and food boxes. When the scene changes on the TV to a brighter one, she catches the quick glint of crumpled foil and bent spoons.

He notices her looking, glances over his shoulder, and then cracks the latch on the screen door, forcing her to step back as he moves out onto the porch, dragging the front door shut behind him. "What, uh—what's up?" The size of his pupils don't change in the dim evening sunlight. He moves like he's underwater, each movement caught against a current she can't see.

"I..." It's not like she can tell him she's over here repenting because she thought for a second that it would be OK if he died, so she says instead, "I need your help."

"Oh." He scratches his stubbled cheek, half-lidded gaze drifting over the street. "Sure," he says. "With what?"

Right, exactly, with what? Roberta turns and gives her property a quick scan, then she points at the plastic flamingo and the tattered whirligigs. "I need you to pull those out of the ground for me. The garbage truck comes tomorrow, so I thought..."

Nodding, he says, "Yeah, OK. No problem, just, uh..." he looks down at the ground, turns as he uses his toes to kick his discarded slip-ons over, "need my sandals here."

He struggles with the flamingo, because Mikey did such a good job staking it into the ground. Tendons strain under track-marked skin, but it only takes a second for him to yank out the whirligigs and then lean all three against the front of her trailer. "Here OK?"

Roberta tears her eyes off them and swallows as she nods. "Sure."

"So... that it? You good now?"

"Yes," she says, fingering the dusty fan of a whirligig. It leaves a smudge on her fingertips that she wipes away on her shirt. "Yes, that's it."

He's turning to go, pulled by that invisible tether Mikey used to be tied to, knot so tight that he once apathetically dragged her down the hallway as she clung to his shirt hem, begging him not to leave. She looks at the drug dealer's trailer. It's a bright, sunny day, and his windows are black. She flicks the whirligig, the one that has enough room against the trailer to still spin, thinking about the way Mikey stood at the edge of the lawn and watched the wind come over them once he was finished staking them in, an expression on his face that she still can't quite place, even though she thinks of that day all the time. She had been watching him from the porch, shouting out directions, but in that moment she'd stood there, silently gripping the railing as she realized there was nothing more she could say to him.

The drug dealer is about halfway across the street when she calls out to him again. "Kid, hey. Wait." When he turns back to her, in the middle of the street with his hands in his pockets, she says, "What you're doing in there..." She gestures to the trailer. "You're gonna kill yourself."

He gives her a limp smile. "What are you talking about, old lady?"

"I know what you're doing in there," she says.

The drug dealer seems to wake, enough for his spine to straighten, to look up and down the street. It's like she said some kind of secret word to activate him. He takes a couple purposeful steps back across the road. "What are you talking about?" he asks again as he stops in front of her.

"I'm talking about the drugs you're doing in there."

She watches his face harden, his lips pressing into a tight line as color blooms up his neck. "Shut the fuck up about that, OK?" he says in a low voice. Again, he checks the street for anyone nearby. "Just shut the fuck up. What I do in my own home is none of your fucking business."

The sputtering well of her goodwill dries up in an instant. She had Mikey's goddamn whirligigs pulled out for this, to get him out of the trailer, to check on him. *He deserves it.* "You're *making* it everyone's business," she spits, "with your dirty rotten 'clientele' running around this place like you're raiding a bloody department store. You and the rest of those crackheads aren't exactly subtle. Strutting around like *this*." She grabs his arm, twisting its underside up.

"Ow, shit!" He wrenches his arm out of her grasp. "What the hell are you—"

"I'm not the clueless old diddy you think I am."

"You *don't* know what you're talking about," the drug dealer says as he starts to back up across the road. "You don't."

She can't tell if that is supposed to be a threat or not, but she still can't seem to help herself because what does it matter now? "And *you* don't know what you're doing to the people who love you, you stupid boy. What you're doing to the families of the people you're selling to. You have no bloody idea the hell you're putting them

62

all through."

The drug dealer throws his hands up. "Yeah, well, you know what old lady, there's no one who would give a shit anyway. OK? So just keep your nosey, gossiping ass out of my business."

Roberta stands at the edge of her yard with her fists tight at her sides as she watches the drug dealer slam his screen door with a metallic clash. She's tempted to run across the street and pull up every single one of his sunflowers. *Stupid son of a bitch why do I even try keep him the hell away from me if this is how it's going to be I can't do this again.*

Throat thick, Roberta struts back to the front of her trailer, and then awkwardly carries all three whirligigs back to the edge of the lawn, where she throws them down into the dead grass. Picking one up, she tries to press its plastic stake into the ground, just past where the old hole is, but it wobbles and bends in her shaking hands, and she can't get it much deeper than an inch. When she releases it, it flops back to the grass like it's spent, like it has no spinning left in it.

So she has no other choice but to stick all three back into their old holes, where they don't stand straight as before, but instead lean crookedly in the still air.

August slips away into September. The grasshoppers come out, springing away from every step with an unexpected flash of yellow wings. The kids start waiting at the edge of the park for the bus again, oversized backpacks hanging loose from small shoulders, and Roberta starts telling time by the screech of air brakes at 7:35 AM and 3:10 PM. The rest of the day is filled with the gravelling drone of lawn mowers grinding away into the afternoons as the water restrictions begin to lift.

Roberta sees more of the drug dealer's customers than the drug dealer himself. She catches her neighbors from #34 and #35 complaining about their park manager and the lack of action against the drug dealer while she is retrieving her pension cheque from her mailbox. She and Tutsi resume their loops around Evergreen Crescent alone. *This is a good thing a prayer finally answered.* Once in a while, though, she will step out into the cool morning to her tomatoes dripping, a damp spot from the draining hose dark against the lighter dust of his driveway.

It is the middle of a Wednesday night when Roberta wakes to the smell of smoke. But it doesn't alarm her like it used to, desensitised after years of carrying on living while everything burns somewhere distant enough to stop noticing. When she opens her eyes, they're so bleary that she doesn't realize at first that the smoke is lingering in her room. She blinks at the streaks of streetlight cutting beams through its haze. She blinks again, rolls onto her back as she watches it hang overhead, still half-asleep, confused. She wonders where it might be burning now. Must be close. *Can't you just let this shit end* because things were finally beginning to die down. Tutsi, usually a tight curl on the end of her bed, is sitting up, his ears perked.

It's when she hears a loud, hollow *pop!* that she sits up, drags herself out of bed, hips stiff as she waddles down the narrow hall into the living room. The smoke gets thicker as she goes. So does the heat. She stops in the mouth of the hall when she sees, through the curtains of her living room window facing the street, an orange light blazing, shifting hues.

When she pulls the curtain back, she wonders whether this is some kind of a dream, the type the prophets had when God was trying to tell them something. Her trailer trash version of the burning bush. Because somehow, for some reason, the drug dealer's trailer is ablaze, flames pouring out of the windows, red plumes of smoke pummeling the sky.

She is ramming her feet into her flip flops as she fumbles with the deadbolt on the front door; she is running out into the street with only her nightgown on. For a moment, Roberta stands paralyzed in the middle of the road, standing in front of the inferno. Just under the roar of the fire, she can hear Tutsi barking from across the street.

Then she notices the hose by her feet. The metal tap burns her hands when she lunges for it, a white hot pain so sharp it feels like a cold electric shock. The hose gurgles to life at the edge of his driveway, and when she picks it up, the rubber is warm and soft between her hands.

64

She turns and aims at the trailer, just as his front window explodes. A gush of flame, like inverted water, pours heavily into the sky. Roberta cries out, ducking to avoid its blast of heat and shards of glass. She staggers away a few steps, then straightens as she aims the hose unsteadily at the flames, pressing her thumb over its unnozzled mouth to get some kind of a spray.

The flames hardly flicker.

She starts trying to soak the steps so she can get to the front door instead. When she opens her mouth to call out to the drug dealer, she realizes she still doesn't know his name. "Kid!" she starts hollering. It's a lot like drowning, sucking in a lungful of smoke. Coughing hard, she warbles, "Kid! Kid, wake up!"

Hot tears are going down her face from the sting of the smoke, but she pushes forward anyway. She's staggered up the three steps of his porch, trying to soak the door enough to try and get in there—*Goddammit no please why please shit it burns please please*—when suddenly there are hands on her shoulders, half-dragging half-carrying her back down the steps.

"No, no!" She starts struggling. "There's someone *in* there—"

"Roberta!" yells a voice in her ear. "Roberta, what the fuck are you doing?"

She turns and looks up to see the drug dealer standing there, still gripping her shoulders. He's looking over the top of her head, at his trailer, his eyes alight in the flame. She can feel its heat against her back. The hose she hasn't let go of is still gushing water, soaking their feet, slapping against the concrete as the sound of sirens prick the air.

He swallows as his gaze drifts again to her. "Are you—were you just—?"

Before Roberta can say a word, a fire truck comes screaming up the street, all bright reds and flashing lights, and then uniformed firefighters descend and surround them.

In the blue light of early morning, Roberta and the drug dealer sit on her porch in the mismatched patio set with blankets around their shoulders, watching the firefighters roll their hoses back up. The ambulance ambles back toward the entrance, slow and silent, almost like it's disappointed not to be carrying anyone away with it.

The park residents, brought out by the commotion and the lights, have also slunk back to their own homes. There was some damage to his closest neighbors, a few darkened patches against their sidings. The maple in #13's backyard is the only one other than Roberta who got hurt. Like her, a few of its arms are burnt, with one that will probably need to be amputated so it doesn't break off and damage anything further.

It's the drug dealer's trailer that is in the worst shape. Though the back of it is still mostly in tack, its front is a skeleton. Its blackened metal frame rears like a ribcage where the fire-weakened siding fell away. She can see the burnt outline of his couch, the walls of the living room and kitchen covered in an ash that looks like a creeping mould. A few crisp, twisted bodies of the drug dealer's sunflowers still stand against its hollow side.

Roberta's hands are bandaged in her lap. "How come you weren't in there?" she asks.

He pulls the blanket tighter around his neck. For the first time, she notices that his eyes are swollen, red cheeks rubbed raw. He has lost more weight since she last saw him, cheeks like pale moon craters. He clears his throat, shrugging. "I don't know. I couldn't sleep, so I figured I'd go get some fresh air. Go for a walk like you and me used to do."

She nods slowly.

"I went around the park a few times... and you said I could say anything, so—when I still had more to say, I just... kept going. I walked all the way to Safeway." He presses the blanket against his eyes and groans. "*God,* you know, I probably looked like a fucking psycho. I'm kicking over people's garbage cans, and then I'm bawling my fucking eyes out. I was just... I was letting him have it, you know? Fuck him, and fuck this, and all that. Fuck everything."

Roberta doesn't know what to say, so she just stares at the trailer's husk.

"Maybe it does piss him off." He tries to laugh, but when he looks at her, all he can do is swallow. "And there you are, trying to put out a house fire with a fucking garden hose."

Before she can say a word, the drug dealer rises from his chair. With his back to her, he swipes his face with the hem of the blanket, and then starts rustling through the tomato plant across from them, the only one that survived her neglect and his attempt to revive them.

"It's Isaac," he says, gently lifting a vine with one hand while the other holds the blanket around his neck like a cape.

"What?"

"My name. Isaac." He turns, and he's got a small red bead between his fingers. "Look."

He holds it out to her, and she cups her bandaged hands to receive it.

Brooke Dreger lives in a small-ish town in British Columbia, Canada. Her work has appeared in other publications, such as *Ekstasis* and *Clayjar Review*.

GLENN ARMOCIDA

The Caretaker of Cemetery Hill

The day fidgeted and squirmed in Tom Leueck's mind like a discontented child as he motored up Mount Springer to his homestead on the outskirt of West Sparrow. He was not a man who gave way to tears when they demanded an exit from his soul and he wondered if there had been any real profit to this approach to life's troubles and eruptions. What good had it done him, he reflected, to push down on that which insisted on pushing up from within, except to enable him to maintain his reputation of strength and stability amongst his family, his employees, his fellow congregants at St. Luke's Church? It wasn't helping him now, he concluded, not after this day.

"How was your day, Mr. Leueck? And leave those boots in the mudroom before you come into my kitchen, please. I mopped the day away and the floors are just how they should look."

"Celia, you know how to wear out a mop." He shed his boots and overalls and strode into the kitchen in his skivvies and work shirt. "Just don't wear out my ears with your bossin'."

"If you're looking to get a rise from me seeing you in your underwear," she said without looking up from the pot she tended on the stovetop, "you know I've seen it all before." She grinned. "And then some."

"I've had a day and a half and I'm glad it's behind me. Wish it was as clean as these floors."

"You can share it with me, if you like, over a bowl of this beef barley stew, which will be ready in half an hour." She embraced her husband and returned to inspect the biscuits in the oven.

Tom showered, shaved, and sat down to his dinner and did not look up from his bowl.

"What is it?" Celia reached her hand onto his thick forearm.

"It's a mess, is what it is. Tom Jr. called off sick so I had nobody, nobody with a brain, that is, to run the hardware side of the store.

Which meant no one to properly reconcile the order we received from the distributor. We may be short a hundred pound of nails and other things. Maybe not. Our youngest showed up with a trophy hangover he won at that bachelor party last night."

"I detest when Dennis drinks like that. He takes after your grandfather, you know."

"I don't need remindin' of that."

"Go on, Mr. Leueck." She buttered a biscuit and set it near his bowl.

"Dennis spent most of the morning in the john." Tom bit off half of the biscuit and chewed. "When he finally got his act together, he discovered that rats had chewed through the alfalfa bin, rat shit everywhere . . ."

"Your language."

He looked up from his bowl, raised his brows, and returned to his stew.

"Well, the rats have ruined that alfalfa." He paused. "Need to get another cat since the store tom lost his fight with that coyote." He swallowed the other half of the biscuit and nodded for another. Celia buttered it and then went to the stove, poured a mug of coffee from the percolator for him and a cup for her, and set them on the oak table built by Tom's grandfather.

"Shane, the young fella I hired, he'll be a good worker when his brains come in. He's been learning to work the loader in the supply yard. Of course, he picked today to forget to shift out of reverse as he was scooping gravel and rammed a customer's pickup."

"Oh, my. You did have a day, didn't you?" She placed her hand on his arm again. "Did the Lord provide anything worthy of the day for you?"

"I think so," he paused over the second biscuit. "Chester Austin and Henry Shick stopped in to get some chicken wire and posts. It was good to see them buddy-buddy again. Guess they kissed and made up." He drained his coffee and set the mug aside. Celia filled it and placed a pan of brownies on the table.

"Look at me, Tom Leueck." He did so. "I love you." She

squeezed his forearm.

"I know it."

"Then the day's not a total loss, now, is it?"

"Close to it. But you always pull my . . . butt out of the fire, Celia." He took her hand and kissed it. "Those things, that's just a routine bad day that comes around. Nothin' to be done about it." He paused. "But this," he fished a letter from his shirt pocket, "this is what made it an award-winning day." He set the letter on the table. "It's from my father to my Grandpap."

Tom rested his head in his hands. Too many times, he thought, the sun had set on the day with one family member or another in the sights of Tom's grandfather and his notorious temper. He knew that his wife understood that all too well, for even Celia, kind and patient and responsible Celia, had once long ago been the target of the old man's invective. But this was different.

"I've seen my share in these seventy-seven years," he muttered, "but nothin' like this."

She looked at the letter and hesitated.

"Go on and read it, ifn you like. It sure explains a lot of things that rotten som'bitch . . ."

"Please."

". . . should've been held accountable for." He dug two brownies from the pan and chewed head down.

"Tom Leuck, please don't talk about your grandfather that way. I know you loved . . ."

"I ain't talkin' about Grandpap."

"Oh? Oh, my." Celia picked up the letter, held it, set it down. She went to the stove for a fresh cup and then took up the letter. While reading it she gasped and looked at her husband, but he worked on the second brownie while staring at the table. She finished the letter, laid it on the table, folded and unfolded and refolded a dish towel, and then read the letter again. She put it back into the envelope and slid it back to Tom. They sat, hard to their own thoughts, each trying to work out what they wished the day had not disclosed to them.

70

"I see." She closed her eyes. "Oh, Tom. I'm so sorry for you." She waited. "The envelope's addressed and stamped . . ." She turned it

over and then back. ". . . but not postmarked."

"Guess he changed his mind and didn't send it. How I read it and the fact that he never mailed it, my father was not only a swindler but a coward, too."

"Where did you find this letter?"

"In the safe at the office. In a file related to the sale of the business in '69." Tom looked up, sipped his coffee, then looked at the ceiling, moving his lips silently, ciphering the years. "Grandpap was eighty-five years old then. My old man would've been fifty-five."

"Will you visit him tomorrow?" She leaned into the table to find his eyes.

"I'll do what I always do on Saturday, my love. There's grass to cut. Stones to be righted."

***

At sunrise the next morning, Tom loaded the 1962 Plymouth station wagon he inherited, the family transport of his youth. He knew his truck would be the sensible vehicle to use and certainly easier to load. But the station wagon served well enough, he reasoned, and its link to his past was a comfort, as were his Saturday duties. He tuned the AM radio to the station in Warren for its Hank Williams program. He crossed Sparrow Bridge onto Route 39 and drove through East Sparrow to Cemetery Hill Road, a tar-and-stone-chip lane that devolved into a gravel and dirt track where the mountain leveled off at the old cemetery. He sat in his wagon, mesmerized, staring at the crumbling, bleached headstones and splintering wooden crosses, the spring wildflowers pushing life up from the dead and nodding in the breeze, as if they were affirming the betrayal that had taken root in his life.

These thoughts dissolved. He reflected that he, too, would die in this Pennsylvania forest and hold the ground until Celia joined him. Their sons, he hoped, would tend to his and Celia's graves as he now tended to the grave of his long-dead, volatile Grandpap, the last

71

person to be buried in this old cemetery, in 1974.

This was his third cut of the new season and the grass was supple and lush now. Honey locust and wild rose washed the air and dandelions arose boasting their pure yellow blossoms. By the afternoon Tom had groomed all twelve rows of twenty gravesites each. He returned to the station wagon, mopped his head with a bandana, loaded his gear, and sat on the tailgate, listening to the ball game in Pittsburgh, fading in and out on the radio's tuner while eating the lunch Celia had packed for him. He finished and snapped closed the lunchpail. He sipped coffee from his thermos and lit his Saturday cigar, and from the flask stashed in the glove box, sipped rye whiskey in between everything else. The letter returned to his thoughts and he leaned and spat, for it left a rancid taste on his tongue and in his heart.

The whiskey settled and arranged his thoughts, something his mind had demanded of him since he discovered the letter, a letter unknown to Tom and that had patiently awaited the proper day to be revealed to him. Another swig of the rye soon gave him the wherewithal to return to 1974, to the hospital in Warren where his grandfather made his last stand, withered, agitated, yet still dangerous in his own way.

The cancer had underestimated the old man's constitution, but it won out eventually, on a January night that came on hard during Tom's watch, the sky blackening by late afternoon and delivering yet another snowstorm. The family took turns standing vigil each day until Grandpap would drive them away with his tongue-lashings, accusations, and vile insults. Only Tom could withstand the onslaught, looking past the cancered man's ravaged countenance into younger days when he kept his inner demon on a shorter leash and took Tom fishing on Sundays after church. They would stop afterward at the East Sparrow Pharmacy to sit at the soda counter to slurp milkshakes together. Grandpap would then tell him to pick out a comic book and gave him the change, solemnly advising young Tom to save the money in the piggy bank he had gifted the boy.

The night nurse sponged the old man indifferently, ignoring

72

his orders to fuck off and leave him be. She took it all in stride, as someone experienced in the futile task of bathing bodies that would very soon expire and have little need for hygiene or grooming. Tom watched as she gently turned his grandfather one way and another to cleanse every passage of his wrinkled, wasted flesh, enduring his groans and outbursts with Job's patience. When she had finished, the nurse took the basin, sponge, and towel into the common bathroom. She washed her hands and emerged only to exit to the hallway and return moments later with a vial and syringe.

"I always check to make sure I'm giving this to the right patient. So, are you Baron Leueck?"

"Well, if I wasn't Baron Leueck I wouldn't be here now, would I?"

"Just a yes or no, please, Mr. Leueck."

"Oh, kiss my ass."

"Mr. Leueck, you've had a rough day. This will take away that horrible pain, help you sleep."

"Where's my whiskey," his grandfather demanded. "I don't need this shit."

"When you go home you can have your whiskey, sir. For now, this will have to do. And we can't mix the two, oh no, no. That would only send you to the grave right quick."

"That's where I'm headed anyways. And you know I'm not going home, you stupid bitch."

"Grandpap, please. Easy, now. Let the nice nurse help you. Let her do her job."

"'Do her job,'" the old man repeated, spitting out the words.

The nurse pushed the needle into the morphine vial, pulled back on the syringe's plunger, draining the vial of its nectar, then pressed the plunger until some of the narcotic squirted out of the needle. She held it to the light and flicked it with her finger to make sure no air remained, and then found a section of vein that had not yet been punctured. A minute later the old man sighed.

Young Tom marveled at the dependability of the opioid, a mere liquid, to alter his grandfather's disposition in but a few minutes.

73

It was during these initial euphoric episodes that the old man was helpless to maintain his junkyard dog nature. Tom would work fast to elicit stories of his youth, his time on the frontlines in Flanders during World War One, and corny jokes that made Tom chuckle for his grandfather's sake.

But the drug's rapture inevitably faded, as it did on this frigid, blasting night, and it took the depleted patient into a twilight, in which he confused past and present, names and years, and the jokes' punchlines.

"A horse walks into a bar and orders a beer," the old man began. He snickered. "The bartender looks at him and says . . . and says . . . oh, shit, what does he say?"

"'Hey pal, why the long face?'" Tom filled in the punch.

"That's it. That's it. Ain't it the funniest thing? Damn, that's good."

A brief slumber followed. Tom, now twenty-seven and working hard to rise in the family business started by Baron and passed to Tom's father, took solace in the old man's painless rest, a man he loved despite his hot blood. Tom moved quietly to the bed to pull the blankets over Grandpap Leueck's hollowed chest and slack shoulders, once the envy of men. He took his comb and worked the thick shock of white hair. He wiped drool from the thin, putty lips and snot from the long thin nose. He kissed his grandfather's forehead.

Tom turned to stare through the window into the teeth of the winter storm that chewed against the hospital and the small city and the rows of mountains that rippled into the distance, as if trying to outrace the storm, yet frozen in place. He knew, somehow, that the Angel of Death had ridden into town on this weather. What would it take, Tom thought, for me to convince Old Reaper to bypass this particular harvest and not return for a few more years? He wanted more time with the man he admired more than anyone. Then again, he conceded, that would be more years of agony for Grandpap. No. Not that. He considered the volumes of pain that a human endured over a lifetime of ninety years. He figured that, would it all happen at once to a man, his body would rupture and disintegrate. When does a person give way to death, he pondered, if it is even his own choice? Already in his short life he had seen people give up on living at ages far junior to his grandfather, surrendering to nature or the hardness of society or to their own demons harbored in collapsing minds. He summoned the Bible proverb: to everything there is a season, a time to live, a time to die. He very much wanted a longer season with Grandpap Baron Leueck, to continue learning the things that constituted endurance, toughness, discernment. But Tom resigned himself that he would have to take the time, and no more, that was offered to him and his elder at this late stage of the battle.

He turned from the window and right into the old man's glare.

"Grandpap, you're awake. Can I get you . . ."

"I know what you did to help my son steal the store from me." His eyes narrowed to slits.

"Sir?"

"Don't 'sir' me, boy. I know what you did."

"What are you saying, Grandpap?"

"Don't you be actin' so innocent, you little bastard. You and that lousy father of yours stole my store from me."

"I don't know what you're talking about." Tom's heart raced and he became dizzy with the confusion and the weight of the accusation sat down hard in his stomach. He approached the bed, a wretched half-smile contorting his face with sympathy and fear. He pushed back on tears now.

"'I don't know what you're talking about.'"

"Grandpap, please . . ."

"You little shit," he bellowed, "I thought I could always count on you . . ."

At this, the depleted man coughed hard, showering his blanket with phlegm, clutched his chest, closed his eyes, and groaned. His breathing labored in opposition to the groans that pealed from his raggedy throat.

75

Tom sprinted to the nurse station at the end of the hall. When he and the nurse returned, the patient did not respond to their prodding. Half an hour later, though, the doctor declared Tom's

grandfather to be as good as could be expected at this stage and just in need of sleep. Tom reluctantly left for home, prompted by the nurse, and wrangled with confusion and pity and remorse all night. And while he did this, Baron Leueck dropped his guard one last time and dropped into a coma. He died alone as the night ended and the winter storm abated.

When young Tom awoke, he watched from his bed as the sun labored weakly over the eastern mountain ridges, pale in the frosted mist that rose from the ancient Allegheny River that wound through the forest. It was as if the morning itself was reluctant to witness the lifeless husk of the old warrior and offered its bleak light as a poor substitute for the ceremony of remembrance.

Tom was shocked to hear a voice, unlike any he had heard before, a voice both in is head and in his ear, proclaim the passing of his grandfather. He sat up and called out to his empty house. He swung his feet to the floor and sat listening to his breathing. As he reached for the shotgun next to his bed, the voice, such as it was, assured him, "Do not fear. Do not waste time arranging the shadows of the past." Tom was suffused in a calm unlike he had ever experienced. He laid back down and stared at the ceiling, contemplating this encounter with what he reckoned could only be the expression of the Divine.

A month after the burial at the old cemetery, Tom confronted his father about his grandfather's deathbed claim. All was attributed to the compounded troubles of the cancer, the morphine, and age.

"Don't take any of that to heart, son," his father dismissed with a wave of his hand. "Your Grandpap was beyond addled at that point. He was probably hallucinatin' from the drug and the dyin'. You rest easy that you done good by him. Which you did more than a body could ask. You know he loved you."

"Easy for you to say. What Grandpap accused me of doin', how can I rest easy?"

"You'll figure it out."

"And the way he said it. Then he just up and died afterward... it hurts like hell."

"Well, maybe it's time for you to finally grow up. Get over it, like a man."

Thirty years slid by and the husband-and-wife team that had tended to the town's original cemetery died. Tom visited his grandfather's grave and, witnessing the decline of the grounds, took it upon himself to serve as caretaker, as no one from the Sparrows bothered to do so. This he continued to do for the past twenty years, most every Saturday.

***

Tom took the flask and the five-gallon whitewash bucket from the trunk and walked to row 5, plot 20 to visit Baron Leueck, who rested next to Tom's grandmother on one side, great-grandparents on the opposite. He turned the bucket upside-down, sat on it, and relit his cigar.

"Grandpap, I don't know nothin' about the dead. Other than they're dead. But I believe you've heard what I've said over the years. I sure as hell hope so."

He pulled on the cigar and sipped the rye. He looked at the headstone and there was the date of death, carved in granite. Just like everyone else's, he mused, just like his would be someday. This chilled him, for he understood the nearness of that date with more import each year now.

"I've got something to share with you. There ain't no good way to explain it." He paused. "And I ain't lookin' for anything out of it. Least I don't think I am?" He pulled the letter from his shirt pocket. "I found this in the safe yesterday. Maybe I should say that it found me. It's a letter from Dad to you, dated in September of '73, exactly four months afore you passed. Anyways, here goes."

September 16, 1974

Poppa,

I hope you'll read this entire letter. I don't like having this enmity between us. Things are ugly. Maybe we can reach an understanding. You're old now—hell, I'm getting old—and you know all about your health and the odds. We don't know the time that remains.

I'll get to the point: I did arrange things to take over the business. I did it without your consent or even knowing of it. And I don't regret it. I'll reckon that right now you're thinking, "I knew it all along." But what you keep forgetting, or choose to forget, is this—you promised to pass the business to me when you reached seventy-five and I turned forty-five. You didn't live up to your word. When I reminded you of it, well, you know what you said to me. You made me wait ten extra years and there was nothing I could do about it. Until I figured out what I could do about it. You were so sharp for so long. But you've always been a damn stubborn man, to a fault. You never wanted to try something new. Just wanted to keep it a feed store, didn't want to expand. I got the hardware section going, and then the building supplies business. They've been solid lines for us, which you can't deny, and which profited you and all of us. It came down to this: I had to take the business for the sake of the business and for your own good. And so you would follow through on your word, even if you didn't know it or didn't want to. And there's nothing you can do about it now.

Something else. I had my Tom sign documents, but he didn't know what he was signing. I told him something or another and just showed him where to sign. Your grandson is innocent in all of this. You got no bone to pick with him. You know he loves you. Hell, he loves you more than he loves me. Leave Tom out of this, it wasn't his doing.

Can we bury the hatchet and patch up?

I sure hope so.

Rick

Tom folded the letter and returned it to his pocket. He sipped from the flask and lit his cigar. He watched a herd of deer—he counted thirty—approach the hilltop along a stretch of choke cherry and sweet birch trees that bordered the cemetery. That's odd, he thought, so many together this time of year and moving during the daylight.

"Grandpap, Dad never mailed this letter to you. He had it in an envelope, addressed and the postage and all. But it's not postmarked

I don't know why he didn't send it. I sure wished that he'd done so." Tom breathed deeply and exhaled slowly, holding onto his nerve. He didn't want the tears now, not in front of his grandfather. "I sure do wish it."

The late afternoon sun slanted through the canopy of the surrounding forest, the mottled shadows flickering across the tombstones and the freshly mown turf, the fertile aroma of the cut grass rising into the warm spring air and its gentle currents that enveloped the caretaker of Cemetery Hill. Tom took this in and closed his eyes, absorbing the goodness of the moment to settle, if for only a spell, the turmoil that unsettled his heart the past two days, turmoil which itself had resurrected the wretched ghost of that January night fifty years ago. He remained this way, on the border of trance and enchantment, and felt the passing of something he could not name across his mind and heart, something that felt perfectly true and good. And then he heard the voice, the same one that had startled him all of those years ago, the morning he awoke and knew his Grandpap had passed through the eternal veil. "Forgive" was all that it said, and he snapped from his reverie.

When he looked up, Tom saw the flock of turkeys, maybe two dozen jakes and hens, feeding along row 1 of the cemetery. He had hunted these large birds enough times to know that their superior eyesight would not have failed them to notice him. Yet, they carried on with their scratching and pecking as if he didn't exist. He ventured a movement, relighting his cigar and drawing from the rye, and the turkeys paid him no mind. Strange days, he concluded, strange indeed.

"Grandpap, I've heard Father Wallace preach on forgiving, not long ago," Tom said. He looked sidewise at the turkeys. They had stopped feeding and were studying him, a gaggle of googly eyes bobbing and jerking, their bluish-red wattles vibrating as they turned their heads.

"Anyways, he made his case, and a good one at that, pointing to Jesus talkin' to Peter about forgiving your brother seven times seventy." Tom paused and glanced at the turkeys again. They continued their watch on him, though some had resumed feeding.

"And I had to agree with him. Well, agree with Christ is a better way to put it. It ain't Father Wallace's command, now, is it? I mean, he's a good enough man, but he's no Jesus." He paused again and drew the cigar smoke and exhaled through his nose. All the turkeys now were once again head to the ground.

"The thing is, how does a body begin into the forgiveness on such a dirty deed? Not just on you but on me, too. He hit us both with one big roundhouse, a knockout. It's a damned shame that I have to call him my father. And now I gotta forgive the man?"

There on the edge of the woods the deer reappeared and stepped into the open, not far from the turkeys. They walked their circles, arranging the grass as they liked, and then bedded down. The turkeys looked around herky-jerky, conferring with one another, and they, too, pulled at the grasses, waddling in small circles, and nested down on the ground.

"Now who in creation is gonna believe this when I tell it?" Tom shook his head. "They must be havin' themselves a convention. I never seen the likes of this."

Tom drained the last of the rye whiskey and looked at the flask. He calculated that it was not possible that this amount of the spirit would have him seeing things like deer and turkeys settling in for a bullshit session. He slid the flask into his hip pocket and then puffed his cigar.

"And the Lord only knows who, or what, got into my head and my ear just now." He pondered this. "Just like the morning you died. Did I ever tell you about that, Grandpap?" He paused. "No? Well, a voice, if that's what one could call it, told me you had died. And I mean the oddest voice I'd ever heard. I'm surprised I hadn't told you this afore. Woke me up, told me you had died. Thought there was someone broke into my house. Now all these years later, it talks to me again, right here, out in the open, not a soul to be seen
Well, no one among the quick, anyways. No offense intended." He thought this over and hunched his shoulders. "Tellin' me to 'forgive.' I know who I gotta forgive." He looked down at his boots and sighed. "But no mention of how I go about such a thing."

80

The series of short, sharp barks and whining yips preceded the emergence of a pack of foxes from the other side of the woods bounding the cemetery and they lolled straight across through the headstones and lay down in the cooling grass. Tom counted twenty-six. He felt the willies run up his spine. He looked around to make sure that bears weren't in the waiting.

"This is the only time I wished I had one of them dumbphones with a camera. Because no one at the Elks or church or anywhere in this county is gonna believe this."

Tom reached for the flask again and, remembering that it was empty, shook his head. He looked out across the river valley, aglow in the gold of the late day sun, and watched as a small dark cloud crossed the river and headed straight toward the hilltop. As it drew closer, shifting and in flux, he saw that it was not a cloud but a large flock of birds. They came in low and noisy and settled in the trees surrounding the cemetery, hundreds of sparrows. Tom reached again for the flask and stopped short.

Carrying through the forest, unnatural in the placid scene surrounding him, came the sound of an engine, growling and changing with each gearshift, and gradually descending on the cemetery from up the hollow. Tom saw the vehicle round the bend, the large, bearded man at the wheel of the all-terrain side-by-side squinting into the low sun. The man sat upright when he spotted Tom, slowed for a moment, and then motored up next to Tom's truck and shut down.

When he stood, stretching away the stiffness of his day's labor and rubbing his butt to relieve the numbness from sitting on the bucket, Tom saw that the deer, turkeys, foxes, and birds all had their eyes directed at the man dressed in hunting camouflage who was now lumbering toward the graves.

"Hey there," the man called out. "Didn't expect to find anyone here. How goes it?"

"That makes two of us. It goes well enough."

They met halfway in a handshake and stood smiling but eyeing each other.

"I've never run into anyone all the times I've worked here,"

Tom said.

"The living don't have much use for the dead once they're in the ground, it seems. Which is a shame, but understandable. Life is not for the timid, death even less so." The large man paused on this, stretched and looked about. "I see you've met my friends," he nodded toward the animals.

"Never seen such a thing in my life. I won't lie. It's made me a tad uneasy."

"You got nothing to fear. The least of our concerns in this world are these creatures."

"I guess you're right. If I recall properly, Scripture does say somethin' about the lions lyin' down with the lambs or some such and that'd be a good thing."

"Indeed, it does. So, you're a man of faith."

"I am. Not in a perfect way. But who is?"

"None of us."

"I'm Tom Leueck." They shook hands again. "I know we've met afore, but I can't place it."

"You own the feed store on Route 39."

"That's right." His father's letter and its revelations protested this claim in his gut. Damn it all, he thought, making me feel like a fraud now. Disdain for his father welled up in his heart again. "Sometimes I consider myself more of a caretaker of the business. Like I am for this cemetery."

"Wade Hallar. Though I've been called other names, most not worth repeating."

"That's it. Your beard threw me off'n the scent. You live the other side of Mount Springer from me, big ol' spread. You have the timber business, with your brother Jack."

"Guilty on all counts, Tom. I was in your store a few times. My cousin has the supply store in Warren and I always got a discount with him, being family and all."

"You did that cut for Dale Spendle a few years back, the plateau near the top of the mount."

"We did. Though I've retired from the logging. Jack runs the show, now. I've moved on to other things."

"I've heard some rumors," Tom began and then looked at his boots. "What I mean to say is . . . some folks doin' some talkin' when maybe they should've kept their mouths shut. Said you became a preacher man. Not at a church. A travelin' preacher."

"Those aren't rumors."

"That's a big change."

"Well, God called me out of the timber business to preach the gospel to everyone in this forest." Wade pulled on his beard and looked around. "And to every creature, too. So, I do it."

Tom puzzled on this and coughed. "You're preachin' to the animals?"

"Yes, sir."

"Not meanin' to be ignorant and such, but . . . why?"

"It sounds odd, I know. But I'm just obeying." He paused and smiled. "Gotta say, they make a great audience. They don't heckle me."

At this, the animals began to grunt, cluck, bark, and chirp. The men looked at each other.

"Sometimes they get impatient. I'd better get started. I've been meaning to talk with the folks here for some time." Wade held up his hand and the animals quieted.

"The folks here?"

"The folks here."

Tom looked around at the rows of gravestones, now golden in the late sun.

"I see. I'm guessin' they won't be hecklin' you, either."

"One can only hope so."

"But . . . they're dead. Ain't it too late for them?"

"I don't know, Tom. Jesus preached the good news to the dead in Hades before he rose on the third day. Guess he was making the best of the situation. I figure if he thought it a good idea, that's good enough for me. Stick around, if you like. There might be something worth hearing."

***

Electric candle lights glowed in each of the windows of the Leueck home by the time Tom parked his station wagon in the garage. He knew Celia would have dinner waiting for him and that she would have eaten hers by now, another Saturday night meal by her lonesome. The regret of missing the mealtime with his wife exceeded all else that weighed on his mind. He knew she had the gift of forbearance and that she exercised it to great lengths. The thought of Celia thinking that he would take advantage of this aspect of her nature bore down on him. *I'm blessed*, he thought as he unpacked his gear, *to have her by my side in this hard world*. He limped into the mud room.

"Boots, please."

Tom stopped and smiled. He sat on the small bench and unlaced.

"You can strip down and shake out your dungarees and socks before you walk into my kitchen. Leave your clothes by the door, Mr. Leueck."

They embraced in the kitchen, kissed, and Tom held on when Celia moved to pull away. They stood, silent in the dusky light, arms across each other's backs. Then he hobbled upstairs and showered and shaved and dressed in pajamas.

"I should've known better than to make stuffed pork chops on a Saturday," Celia lamented, "it being your extra-late day." She poured coffee for them both, then ladled gravy over his dinner plate. "If they're dried out, I'm only half-sorry for it." She sat and watched him eat, examining his face for clues to his heart. She knew it was damaged and aching and this drove away what remained of her agitation.

"They're fine, Celia. 'Delicious' puts it far better."

She buttered a slab of her sourdough bread and held it toward him. He reached without looking up from his plate and she did not release it. Tom looked at her.

"Some bread for your thoughts." She held onto the slice.

"At the moment, I'm thinkin' I'd sure like to eat your homemade bread. I've got a hunger."

"Not fair. There's something. It's all over your face." She

84

released the slice and leaned into the table. "Talk to me, Tom Leueck."

"I'm just tired is all."

"You're later than usual. Not that I'm one to keep tabs on my husband. Did you do more than cut the grass and reset headstones?"

Tom set his fork on the plate. He sipped the coffee and then, elbows on the table, his head on his fists, stared back into the day. *Where to begin*, he mused.

"I sat with Grandpap longer than usual." He paused. "I read the letter to him. I'm guessin' he turned over once or twice. Could almost hear him growling, 'Tell me something I don't know.'"

"You did right, Tom. Whether he heard it or not . . . I'll take your word on it." Celia reached her hand onto his arm. "Did it help you some?"

"Some."

After he finished his meal, Celia washed the dish and silverware, humming lowly. Her husband, she knew, took time opening his mind to her. She returned to the table with two plates of cherry pie. They ate in silence, each turning over in their minds what they knew of the day.

"Something happened there. Actually, some things happened. I don't know where to begin so I'll start at the beginning."

"No one should underestimate your wisdom, Tom."

"And no one should underestimate your persistence, my love. You'd have made a good bloodhound." They reached for each other's hand.

"After I read the letter to Grandpap, I was pretty worked up. Or down, is a better way to put it. I felt . . . helpless. I hate that."

"Who doesn't?"

"No one more so than me," he continued. "And while I was settin' there, with everything weighin' on me . . . his accusation, his dyin' alone, and all these years carryin' it around inside, the letter . . ." He paused and looked into her eyes and then at the table and back into her eyes. "Well, then somethin' happened inside of me. Somethin' hard to describe. But it was a peaceful thing, whatever it was. A good thing." He paused and swallowed hard. "Then this voice comes out of

85

nowhere tellin' me, 'Forgive'."

"A voice?"

"A voice."

"Who was it?"

"There wasn't anyone, Celia. As I breathe, it just came out of the air."

Now they gripped each other's hand tighter.

"'Forgive.'"

"'Forgive.' That's what it said to me."

"Forgive what?" Celia pressed.

"It's not a 'what'. It's 'who.'"

"All right, then. Who are you . . . oh, I see."

"T'was the same voice I heard the morning Grandpap died. I told you about that." She nodded. "Unlike any voice I've heard afore. Today, it spoke to me again. Told me to 'forgive.'"

"Oh, my. You've been touched, Tom. That was God's Spirit talking to you."

Tom wiped his mouth, excused himself, and went out to the garage. He lit a cigar and paced out into the driveway and back through the garage and back out, as if tracking all the elements of the day that his mind found so inexplicable and so elusive to trap and hold down and inspect. Even so, how could he understand these things, he lamented, when his heart was so damned heavy, so full of what he could not bring himself to name, other than to call it 'father?' After a dozen laps, he returned to the kitchen. Celia had finished her kitchen work and sat at the table with a fresh cup of coffee. She poured one for Tom and they sat together again.

"Now, the other things. I met a man up there today. Wade Hallar. Him and his brother have the timber business the other side of this mountain. Well, he's out of that, now."

"He was visiting relatives in the cemetery?"

"No." Tom inhaled deeply and looked away. "He came to preach."

"Preach? To who?"

"To the folks buried there."

86

Celia closed her eyes. The grandfather clock in the dining room gonged 9 o'clock and then a deeper silence filled the kitchen. She rose and walked to the window, shaking her head, then returned and stood, staring at her husband.

"Are you OK, Tom?"

"I am." He paused and wondered where to go with this report. "I watched him do it. He stood up on one of the benches and preached to the dead."

"I see." Celia sat and began folding a stack of kitchen towels. "Did they offer 'amens?'"

"The strangest thing about it all . . ."

"Are you saying there's something stranger than preaching to the dead?"

"He preached to the animals, too. They came to the cemetery, lots of 'em. Couple dozen each of deer, turkeys, foxes. Hundreds of birds, sparrows. He said they come to him wherever he is preachin'."

"I knew I smelled the rye on you, Mr. Leueck." She took the next towel to fold, shook it hard so that it snapped, and slapped it down on the table. "How ever did you drive home properly?"

"I weren't drunk, Celia." Tom stepped carefully. "I can't say I was straight as a pin. But I weren't drunk." He watched his wife now folding the towels like a military drill sergeant. "You know me better than that. Ifn I was drunk, I would've slept it off and then drove."

"Well, then," she sniffed, "you know what you're doing, grown man and all. Go on."

"Don't be cross with me, my love. You asked if there was somethin' and I've told you. I read the letter to Grandpap. That, whatever it was, inside of me. The voice tellin' me to forgive. Saw a man preach to the dead and the animals." He winked. "Just another day." Celia kept folding towels and Tom's smile faded.

"You've had a day, no doubt. Even if it was sullied by the whiskey. So, what did he preach?"

"It's not left my thoughts. I'm still ciphering it. He talked about God's om . . . omni . . . oh, what's that word?"

87

"Omnipotence?" Celia looked at him sideways and raised her eyebrows.

"That's it. What you said. Anyways, he went on and most of it made sense. But I wasn't familiar with the Scripture he quoted and it's puzzled me to no end. I asked him to write it down."

Tom pulled a scrap of paper from one pajama pocket, his reading glasses from another, and reached for a Bible from the kitchen bookshelf. He flipped through the book back and forth, sighed, turned to the table of contents, found the passage, ran his finger down a page and recited.

"*Who has ascended into heaven, or descended?*
Who has gathered the wind in His fists?
Who has bound the waters in a garment?
Who has established all the ends of the earth?
What is His name, and what is His Son's name?
"It's a passage from . . ." Tom began.

"The Old Testament. Proverbs 30," Celia finished for him. She snapped and pressed and folded the last towel.

"Chapter and verse. That's my Celia. What do you think it means?"

"It's a challenge by the writer to acknowledge God's power." She placed the towels in a cabinet next to the table. "His omnipotence. Your word of the day." She smiled. "If he can do those things, what can't he do, is what it means."

They sat in silence again, forming and reforming their thoughts of the past two days, connected by their vows, two people but one body for fifty years of marriage, and yet disconnected by the letter that tore apart what they had thought they knew of their family. Tom bowed his head, chin to chest, sighed from the weight of the letter's words that hung across his heart and soul, and wiped his eyes across his sleeve.

Celia rose and stood next to Tom, hand on his shoulder.

"I wish I could take it all from you, Tom, if even for just a day. I know I can't do that. But I'll take as much as you'll allow me to carry for as long as you need me to." She bent and kissed him. "I'm filling in to lead the women's group tomorrow before the service. I'm going to bed. Good night." And another kiss. She started up the steps, stopped, and returned to the kitchen.

"I know you know what you have to do. It's the 'how to do it' that's got you. But I think the answer is right under your nose, Tom Leueck."

Tom listened to his wife ascend the stairs to their bedroom. He sat a long time at the table. Then he went to the garage to finish his Saturday-night cigar. He walked circuits from inside the garage to the driveway and back, a trail of smoke tracing his steps, thinking about how he would go about such a thing as holding the winds in his hands, or wrapping the oceans and seas in a coat, or forgiving his father.

Glenn Armocida resides in western Pennsylvania. His first book, *Tales of East and West Sparrow and Other Stories*, will be published in the summer of 2025 by Atmosphere Press. He was a finalist in the Rash Award in Fiction (2024 and 2022). His recent work appears in *The Broad River Review, Black Moon Magazine, Havik, The Watershed Journal*, and *The Ground Up*. In the 1980s, Glenn attended the University of Pittsburgh as an English major in the Creative Writing Program. During this time, he published poems in various journals and feature articles in *Pittsburgh Magazine, Pittsburgh Post-Gazette*, and *Executive Report*. He has worked as a mill laborer, cook, radio news anchor, printer, technical and business writer, editor, and the past 33 years as an investment manager. When he is not writing, Glenn is with his family, serving the homeless, tending his gardens, or pursuing outdoor life.

HOMILIES

MARK D. STUCKY

Defending the Doubting Disciple
Based on John 11:7–8, 16; 20:24–29

Bad Nickname?

Many people receive a nickname at some point in their lives, which usually reflects more about the individual who *names* than the individual *named*. Nicknames are sometimes terms of endearment, but undesirable nicknames smear and humiliate people.

One such nickname about a biblical character was applied to the misunderstood disciple called "Doubting Thomas." He's not named that anywhere in the Bible, but his infamous doubt later became synonymous with his name.

During Sunday School as a kid, I had the impression that Thomas was an inferior disciple, not as evil as Judas, of course, but surely worse than the other ten. I thought this because doubting was bad, or so I was led to believe.

But I was wrong. Today I believe that Thomas was a disciple of a true committed faith and that doubt itself is misunderstood. Let us first reconsider the nature of doubt.

Having Doubts, Like It or Not?

We can find various verses in the Bible that denounce doubt. Church culture through the centuries has further disparaged doubt. But has all that judgment made doubts go away?

We think we shouldn't have doubts, but we *do* have doubts— doubts about God's love, power, goodness, or mere existence. We doubt our salvation, our motivations, our intentions, our faith, our abilities, our wisdom, our calling. For all our many doubts, Thomas became an unwitting and unwanted role model.

People may desire money, power, and various other temptations, but nobody ever craves having more doubts. We can't seem to extinguish or evade doubts. They lurk around dark corners eager to nip at our heels.

Church traditions condemn what we don't want but can't avoid. What do we get when "righteous" condemnation combines with massive quantities of the very thing condemned? Guilt, and lots of it. Guilt that erodes our wellbeing, like battery acid corroding terminals under the hood of faith.

We don't need to feel guilty. Having doubts is OK and part of normal human experience. Not only that, but in some cases having doubts is even a *good* thing, not a bad thing.

Evil Trap or Tool for Good?

Doubt does not equal unbelief. Having doubt is both believing and *not* believing at the same time. We believe something, but there is some questioning inextricably jumbled up with it. That mixture's relative percentage varies as time goes by. Few people believe things 100 percent without the smallest question, all the time, 24/7. If the questioning percentage nears zero, we easily overlook the doubt. If the balance is closer to 50/50, then doubt is hard to ignore.

James 1:8 describes doubt as being double-minded. Doubt is having a foot in each of two different boats of thoughts or beliefs. While both boats are docked or are moving in parallel, one can tolerate not fully being in one or the other. But when the boats diverge, when the gap over the choppy waters widens, when we feel pulled apart, then doubt becomes a crisis.

But a crisis is both dangerous and an opportunity. Daniel Taylor wrote in his book *The Myth of Certainty*, "Normally doubt is seen as sapping faith's strength. Why not the reverse? Where there is doubt, faith has a reason for being. Clearly faith is not needed where certainty supposedly exists, but only in situations where doubt is possible. . . . Doubt makes its claims, even daily, and they are respected, but they do not determine the character of my life."[1]

A. J. Conyers similarly wrote, "It is not in certainty that a person grows toward a stronger trust in God. Where understanding ends, and we admit to it, we experience 'doubt.' Doubt struggles against that limit, and calls out to God for the answer. Doubt searches for solutions where none are apparent. Doubt . . . is the opportunity for faith. It stands at the edge of past understanding and searches for more."[2]

Everybody doubts at times. It doesn't matter what one does or doesn't believe. Even atheists can doubt their faith in the *non*existence of God. Contrary to the general idea that doubts lead people *away* from faith, doubts have sometimes done the opposite.

In the seventeenth century, the French mathematician and philosopher René Descartes wrote a devastating critique about certainty of knowledge. He used doubt as a tool to find truth, to discount all things that were not certain. He even had doubts about his own existence and wondered if he might be hopelessly deluded. He doubted *everything* until he got down to the one fact he felt could not be doubted. That one irrefutable idea was the famous phrase: "I think, therefore, I am." This meant the very existence of Descartes's thoughts proved that he himself must exist, and his own thoughts provided a toehold for broader belief. Descartes then developed a philosophical proof for the existence of God, and the existence of a supremely perfect being provided a foundation for believing other things. For Descartes, doubt led to God.

Doubt-filled skeptics are cautious about believing anything without convincing evidence. When skeptics are converted, we know an abundance of truth must exist at the core of that experience.

C. S. Lewis, who wrote the *Chronicles of Narnia* among many other works, was one of the most famous Christian writers of the twentieth century, but in his younger years, he was an atheist. He recalled in his biographical book *Surprised by Joy* that one evening (while he was still an atheist), he was astonished by one conversation with a friend. They were talking about evidence for the historical truthfulness of the Gospels. His hard-core atheist friend admitted that the evidence was surprisingly good and that Jesus may really have died and risen again after all. Lewis was shocked by his friend's admission. Lewis wondered if this "cynic of cynics, the toughest of toughs"[3] was not truly firm in his disbelieving convictions, then where could Lewis turn? Was there no escaping God?

Someone who was a confirmed atheist decades longer than Lewis was Antony Flew. He was the son of a Methodist minister and theologian, but by the age of fifteen, he stopped believing in God. For the last half of the twentieth century, he was a famous atheistic philosopher, but late in life in the early twenty-first century, he couldn't keep believing that the complexities of biological life and the universe occurred just by random chance. He scandalized his colleagues when his doubts led him to conclude there must be a God after all.

Thank God for doubters and skeptics and persons with shaken faith. For if they can believe, so can we all find faith.

Faith or Foolishness?

Faith, to be clear, is not doubt's opposite. The opposite of doubt is gullibility, believing in anything without proper analysis, without hesitation, or without a shred of evidence. Gullible people get deceived by quack medicines, marketing scams, conspiracy theories, con artists, cult figures, and false messiahs. For such people, more doubt would be valuable.

Doubt can be a divine tool to help discern truth from error and faith from foolishness. Between faith and foolishness is a fuzzy borderline . . . and I've blundered across that boundary too many times in my life. Doubt and faith form the checks and balances for safely navigating the spiritual path.

Many people have a false view of not only doubt, but also of faith. Mark Twain said, "Faith is believing something you know ain't true." Unfortunately, many people unconsciously have this view of faith. Certainly, some people *do* believe things that aren't true. However, they don't *know* they aren't true since they believe that they are.

A better theologian than Twain was Blaise Pascal, a

seventeenth-century scientist and philosopher. He wrote, "Faith embraces many truths which seem to contradict each other."[4] Many truths *seem* to be contradictory. Scientists puzzle over the paradoxical nature of light, which acts like waves in some experiments but like particles in other experiments. The wave-particle duality of light is just one example of all the paradoxes in the universe. Faith holds the twin sides of paradoxes together, whether it's light as both wave and particle or Jesus as both God and human.

Faith is a *good* thing . . . *if* it's faith in the *right* thing. Faith in the *wrong* thing steers people down dark roads. Faith without any doubts is blind faith. People without doubts may see everything in simplistic black-or-white terms, judge others by their own flawed code, and believe God is always on their side.

The Bible and history bleed stories of those who *thought* they were doing God's will in battling evil. For mistaken "righteous" causes, humanity has experienced far too many persecutions, inquisitions, insurrections, genocides, lynchings, "just" wars, and never-ending displays of intolerance and malice toward others.

Christians have often said "if only the world had more faith," but maybe we should wish "if only the world had more doubt" because the greatest crimes against humanity were done by those who seemed to have no doubts about what they were doing. In such cases, if those people would have had just a few more doubts about the rightness of their cause, would have had a few more doubts about the correctness of condemning, oppressing, torturing, or killing for their cause, those doubts would have prevented so much suffering.

True-Faith Thomas?

Unfair and untrue is the reputation of Thomas as a faithless disciple. Thomas was not naïve and gullible. He was a skeptic grounded in reality. He didn't want to believe something just because it would make him feel better. He wanted an authentic faith that wasn't wish fulfillment. He wanted the truth at any cost.

And he was ready to pay the cost. On the last trip toward

Jerusalem before the crucifixion, while other disciples felt apprehensive, Thomas faithfully planned to follow Jesus to the death. "Let us also go," he said to his fellow disciples, "that we may die with him."[5]

If Thomas had been a person of weak faith, that could have been the time to hastily depart from the band of disciples. The foreseeable outcome seemed hopeless. Cutting his losses at that point and leaving would have been a logical thing to do. But, despite doubts about their future, he was ready to go and die with Jesus. He acted courageously despite his doubts, and indeed, in Jerusalem, his fears became a reality.

After the death of Jesus on the cross, however, others soon told him a seemingly impossible story that Jesus was alive again. Thomas felt despair but refused to believe outrageous rumors, false reassurances, delusions, hallucinations, or mere myths. He wanted *only* the truth, not foolishness or fantasy.

Thomas, like all of us, would have loved a happy ending, but we all know that Disney-like happy endings are rare in real life. Therefore—quite reasonably, considering the horror he had witnessed—he wanted physical proof that the good news was not too-good-to-be-true news.

A week later, Jesus gave Thomas the answer he was looking for by bodily appearing to him. When Thomas found the truth he was looking for, he confessed, "My Lord and my God." This is the most elevated description of Jesus by any disciple. This courageous seeker of deep truth finally believed and understood Jesus for who he really was.

I think Thomas has been slandered for centuries and we collectively owe him an apology. I think perhaps "*Doubting* Thomas" should instead have the nickname "*True-Faith* Thomas." As we wrestle with our own doubts and uncertainties, let us also, like Thomas, bravely seek true faith.

[1] *The Myth of Certainty* (Downers Grove: InterVarsity, 1992) 81.
[2] "When Doubt Can Help You," *Christianity Today* (3 Feb. 1984) 35.
[3] *Surprised by Joy* (New York: Harcourt Brace & World, 1955) 224.
[4] *Pensées: Thoughts on Religion* (Chicago: Letcetera, 2015) 280.
[5] John 11:16.

After initially studying engineering in college, **Mark D. Stucky** completed degrees in religious studies, pastoral ministry, and communications. After being a pastor, he moved into communications and has been a technical and freelance writer. During his day job, he documented diverse technology products. In his free time, he's written articles, stories, and poems on a variety of (usually spiritual) topics. He has received four dozen writing and publication awards. Mark believes in following facts and faith, understanding other perspectives, preserving the earth, protecting the vulnerable, and saving the world one word at a time (or at least trying to). For more writings and information, see spiritwhispersbymarkstucky.substack.com.

Laura Howard

The Courage to Know

In the beginning, we heard. "Let there be," he said, and we were. And ever since, the call has been to hear. "Hear, O Israel." "Whoever has ears, let them hear." We're called to *obedient* hearing, of course. I learned in a Hebrew class that the Hebrew word *shema* means both "hear" and "obey." Hearing God and obeying God aren't supposed to be separate. Ideally, we obey in the same moment we hear.

But we do separate hearing and obeying, against which the New Testament is full of cautions. I grew up singing a song about Jesus's warning that those who hear his words and practice them are "like a wise man who built his house on the rock," and those who hear and yet don't practice his words are "like a foolish man who built his house on sand." James urges us in his letter: "Do not merely listen to the word, and so deceive yourselves. Do what it says."

Jesus and James talk like obeying is the hard part. First Abraham heard God tell him to sacrifice his beloved son Isaac, and then Abraham had to do it. The second part was the hard part, right?

But for me, that first part, the hearing, is where the fear and trembling comes in. How do I know I've heard God? In my consciousness, my desires, my drives—what's God's? What's mine? I worry that to put any of my ideas in God's mouth would be idolatry.

It feels easier to tell God and myself apart when we're at odds. Maybe it was easy for Abraham to know it was God telling him to kill his son because Abraham didn't want to do it. Upon hearing a word like that, I wonder how I could tell God's voice from the devil's. And how do I tell God's voice and my own when we're *not* at odds? (Do I need to be able to?) Surely, hopefully, sometimes we're not.

If my hermeneutics classes have taught me anything, it's that I tinge every message I receive by my very reception of it. And yet, many scholars of interpretation—and I with them—want to acknowledge that we *can* be shaped by what we've sought to interpret. We're not

99

all echo chambers; ideas from outside of us can change us, even as we meet them from our particular worldviews, cultures, and headspaces. A text and its reader can work on each other. Scholars refer to this process encountering and being encountered by a message as the hermeneutical circle. Good interpretation requires caution, but with time and care, we can spiral towards understanding.

Still, I tire of testing the spirits. I long to hear from God directly, in an immediate—that is, *unmediated*—sort of way. I long to take the interpretation out of it. I long to take *me* out of it.

My mediators—Scripture, sacraments, the church body, and so on—can't save me from myself here. They all come back to me in the end. So I keep on longing to know God "directly," to be able to recognize him in the Bible, beyond the Bible, in the preacher's message, beyond the preacher's message, in the stillness of prayer, in the movement of life. I long to do it all by my lonesome. Priesthood of believers and all that—something I like to think I'm sure my Baptist upbringing got right.

I felt myself a priest-believer early. I remember feeling forlorn on a church trip when I was eleven, leaning against the cool window of the charter bus, a sunbeam on my lap and being sure it meant God's love for me. I remember sitting in the back of the darkened sanctuary when I was twelve knowing for the first time Jesus was asking me to invite him into my weakness like Paul did. I remember praying at fourteen that God would save my friend from suicidal thoughts and self-harm, and when she recovered after some long years in which we both felt sustained by God, I called it an answer to prayer. I remember attending a conference at fifteen, an invitation for each of us to ask God whether we had a call to ministry, and with the faith of a child I was sure I did.

I've come away from turning inward with words too uncomfortable to claim as my own; I've been caught up in visions in my mind's eye; I've felt the holy ghost of a hand on my shoulder. Sometimes within, sometimes without, a humming or a glowing or a diagonal line in my chest or a thread running through my body. Always a writing on the wall of my heart, in the dirt of my thoughts, and I can't wipe the words away until I listen to what's always kinder and harder to hear than anything I'd come up with without him, if I could ever experience such a thing. I don't know how to voice how I've known but I know that I have, that I do. I believe.

But my thoughts keep churning. Lord, help my unbelief! I'm dizzy and half worried I'll wear the hermeneutical circle right out. I swear, I'm not half so daunted by the task of obeying God as I am by the task of hearing him in the first place, of recognizing him, of knowing which call to answer.

St. Augustine writes about God's giving us a prevenient grace (literally, "grace that comes before") that allows us to accept further grace. The ability to choose God is itself a gift from God. Pastor John Ames, protagonist of Marilynne Robinson's novel *Gilead*, remarks to his son that God must also give us "a prevenient courage that allows us to be brave." That seems right to me. And I need a knowledge that would allow me to know, a trust that would allow me to trust. I need God to give it to me. I've got naught but prevenient doubt.

My trust of self was undermined early. Total depravity meant my heart was wicked, my desires sinful, my flesh deceitful. I've been that way since birth—before birth, even. Everything about me bends away from God. The plants that grow toward the light have got something figured out I don't, I thought. But I couldn't trust my thoughts! I'm human, for one thing; a woman, for another. My fundamentalist Christian high school told me women have deficient rational capacities—that's why women aren't supposed to be leaders, aren't supposed to teach the things of God, aren't supposed to mediate anyone else's relationship to God, and need a man to mediate theirs. To doubt the veracity of this was to prove them right. I could believe whatever I wanted about myself; they, the men, might not know all, but at least knew better.

I made the mistake of telling a teacher at that school about the prompting I felt at that conference, that pull toward vocational ministry. "Women aren't called to ministry," she said. Confused, I explained that I had sensed God call me. She was quick to insist: "That was Satan's voice, not God's. You're deceiving yourself."

101

I don't want to deceive myself! The thought that I could spend my time straining for Yahweh and dial into my flesh instead, let alone the devil—little frightens me more.

So I've erred on the side of suspicion. I've spent time more time on my knees trying to delineate me from God from Satan than I have actually submitting, actually petitioning, actually receiving God's presence and anything else he might want to give me.

When Jesus talks about being the good shepherd, he says the sheep "follow him because they know his voice." He says his sheep will run from a stranger, not follow one. And I know, if my mom called me on the phone right now, I'd know it was her, without caller ID or her self-identification. Never have I ever had to stop to debate whether I've heard her or someone else. Jesus says "they do not know the voice of strangers."

Why do I expect Satan's voice to sound indistinguishable from God's? from mine? If I'm someone who prays, God's child, shouldn't Satan sound like a stranger?

Why do I think I can bang on God's door only for him to let Satan open it instead? Jesus says, "Ask, and it will be given to you; search, and you will find; knock, and the door will be opened for you." There's a lot I don't know about what that verse means for us. But the barest meaning I can eke out is that if I bang on God's door, *he* will open it. "Is there anyone among you who, if your child asked for bread, would give a stone? Or if the child asked for a fish, would give a snake? If you, then, who are evil, know how to give good gifts to your children, how much more will your Father in heaven give good things to those who ask him!" Can I count on Jesus to give me his presence when I beg for it?

Don't I always already have it?

In Baptist circles like the one I grew up in, the women-in-ministry debate is mostly about the pulpit: does she qualify to preach? At the Anglican church I attend now, the debate is all about the altar: does she qualify to offer the body of Christ, broken for you, the blood of Christ, cup of salvation, to the congregation? In my view, the answer has to be yes. We Anglicans talk about how sacraments are all about what God is doing in the bread and wine, not about what any humans are doing. In him there is no male or female, anyway.

I didn't think the first time I received Eucharist from a woman would feel like a big deal to me, having already sat under her preaching. From a Baptist point of view, the preaching was the *much* bigger deal. But when Mother Natalie placed the bread in my cupped hands, I wept. I felt like I was receiving Christ in a new way. For once it could've been me in her place, receiving him to offer him to someone else. I felt that to receive his body from a woman was to taste the truth that he is mine without any mediation, a truth I didn't know I wasn't living.

The thing about needing Christ mediated for you is that that means Christ is only for you when someone else is for you. In that little building I could digest it for the first time: *Jesus is for me,* no matter who's against me. And I need to be able to rest in that without qualifiers about any sinfulness or rational (in)capacities or guilt or inherent enmity with God.

Jesus is for me.

And now we can talk about obedience, the danger of hearing without obeying. But not before. If I keep erring on the safe side, supposing it's not him calling me beloved after all, resisting where he's drawing me for fear of failing to go where he goes—that's the most dangerous state of all.

I wrote earlier that Scripture, sacraments, the church body all come back to me, in the end. The grace must be that God keeps coming back to me in the end, too, within these things and without. I want to stop trying to rend the two of us apart. To follow the one who chases after me with goodness and mercy requires, as it turns out, that I trust myself. At least a little.

Laura Howard is a writer based in Wheaton, Illinois. She holds a BA in Philosophy and Biblical & Theological Studies from Wheaton College and an MDiv from the University of Chicago. Laura's work has appeared in Ekstasis Magazine, Christianity Today, and *BitterSweet Monthly*. You can find and follow her work at her Substack: Let Me Be Heavy.

www.ingramcontent.com/pod-product-compliance
Lightning Source LLC
Chambersburg PA
CBHW050903180626
46814CB00007B/2868